Library of
Davidson College

THE HUMAN FACE OF SOCIALISM:
*The Political Economy of
Change in Czechoslovakia*

THE HUMAN FACE *of* SOCIALISM:

The Political Economy of Change in Czechoslovakia

BY GEORGE SHAW WHEELER
*Corresponding Member
Czechoslovak Academy of Sciences Prague
(on leave)
Department of Economics
Washington State University*

LAWRENCE HILL and COMPANY
New York • Westport

Copyright © 1973 George Shaw Wheeler

All rights reserved

ISBN 0-88208-039-3

Library of Congress catalogue card number: 72-96594

First edition May 1973
Lawrence Hill & Company, Publishers, Inc.

Manufactured in the United States of America

To the splendid men and women
of Czechoslovakia
who led the way
to a higher stage of socialism.

"The great basic thought that the world is not to be comprehended as a complex of ready-made *things,* but as a complex of *processes,* in which the things apparently stable no less than their mind-images in our heads, the concepts go through an uninterrupted change of coming into being and passing away—this great fundamental thought has, especially since the time of Hegel, so thoroughly permeated ordinary conscience that in this generality it is scarcely ever contradicted. But to acknowledge this fundamental thought in words and to apply it in reality in detail in each domain of investigation are two different things."

Frederick Engels, *Ludwig Feuerbach,*
English edition, 1946, p. 52. Emphasis in original.

Table of Contents

PREFACE	xi

CHAPTER 1
The Inevitability of Change — 1

CHAPTER 2
The Institutional Background — 6

"Dictatorship of the Proletariat"	10
Central Planning	16
Administrative Price Setting	21

CHAPTER 3
Economic Growth — 25

Agriculture	28
Industrial Development	33

CHAPTER 4
Breakdown in the Efficiency of Centralized Management — 39

Decline in the Efficiency of Investment	39
Waste of Capacity	48
Waste of Materials	52
Productivity of Labor	56

CHAPTER 5
Reasons for the Failure of Centralized Management — 61

Market Competition and Central Planning	66
Competition and Change	71
Encouragement of Quantity Rather than Quality	75
Central Price Fixing Inhibits Change	78
Necessity of Incentives for Change	83
Cost Accounting	96
Education	101

CHAPTER 6
The System of Decision-Making and the Structure of Power — 108

Management Responsibility	108
Inspection, Controls, and Responsibility	114
Censorship	116
Dictatorship and Alienation	119
The Trials and Rehabilitation	121

CHAPTER 7
The "New System" — 126

Clearing the Road for Advance	126
The Action Program	137
The Economic Program	143
The First Results	147

CHAPTER 8
The Intervention — 151

The Warsaw-Brezhnev Doctrine	153

CHAPTER 9
Aftermath—But No Epitaph — 159

CONCLUSION	165
INDEX	171

Preface

The events in Czechoslovakia during 1968 were among the most dramatic and significant of any since the end of World War II.

Understandably, they have been the focus of world attention. Seldom, if ever, have the problems of a small country been discussed by so many for so long and with such a torrent of words. Seldom, if ever, has there been such ill-informed, unscientific, and even deliberately mendacious reporting and analysis. Rarely have so many indulged in such wishful thinking and so many others succumbed to unjustified fears. Emotions mounted and reason fled out the window. Some rejoiced in thinking that socialism was being strengthened; others thought that a return to capitalism was under way. Charges of counterrevolution and anarchy were made, and in the end, military power cut short the political-economic experiment. The immensity of the military force was overwhelming but it solved none of the problems which gave rise to the experiment.

The Czechoslovak people were indeed making one of the most fundamental experiments that mankind can make. They were trying to move socialism ahead from the stage of "dictatorship of the proletariat" to a more humane, democratic, and, not incidentally, a more efficient model. Was this attempt misguided, and even marked by elements of deliberate counterrevolution, as the Five Warsaw Letter Parties* have charged and many people of all shades of opinion believe? Or was it one of the most hopeful developments in many years, an exhilarating experience, yet one based on long and sober scientific analysis, combined with a profound faith in the intelligence, political maturity, and integrity of the country's working people and intellectuals?

These are basic questions not only for Czechoslovakia and

---

* The leaders of the Communist Parties of the Soviet Union, the German Democratic Republic (East Germany), Poland, Hungary, and Bulgaria who met in Warsaw and issued a letter of warning to the Czechoslovak Party on July 4, 1968.

other socialist countries, but also for the relations between capitalist and socialist countries.

If we are concerned with survival, and even the cynics must be, we should try to limit such controversy and to contribute to understanding its primary origins so that perhaps we may find a way out of these acute and almost terrifyingly complex problems. We must start with the facts, emphasizing events leading to 1968. In this study I have made extensive use of quotations, and I believe that the reader will be rewarded by careful attention to them. Their use allows the Czechoslovak leaders of the Communist Party and government to speak for themselves, and the quotations convey the essence of statements and documents of great historical importance. At the same time the references given for each quotation permit the readers to go to the full original sources.

The selection of these quotations does not imply that the person quoted originated the idea or policy. In fact dozens of Czech and Slovak economists, educators, writers, and many others have worked on the problems that are discussed here. There was great depth in leadership of the reform movement. In a very real sense the persons quoted can be said to have responded to the demands for change on the part of nearly the entire population—a population very unusual for the high level of its education and social mindfulness.

Although I believe that scientific arguments should be judged on their merit and not according to the lineage of the author, readers also have a right to know who is speaking to them. I was born in Tacoma, Washington, U.S.A., in 1908. After working on our small farm in eastern Washington I went to Reed College in Portland, Oregon, majoring in economics. There I met and married Eleanor Mitchell, born in Alaska and majoring in political science and statistics. In 1930 we began postgraduate studies at the University of Chicago, witnessing the Great Depression and the near-collapse of the economic system. In 1934 we moved to Washington, D.C., and for the next decade I was a government economist studying various industries in all parts of the United States. Then during World War II I became involved in formulating postwar antifascist policy for Germany and Japan. In 1944 while in England with the "Top Secret" Control Council, I received notice from the United States Civil Service Commission that I had been declared ineligible "because of too friendly feelings for a certain foreign power to hold a key policy-making position." Upon appeal I was allowed to stay, but as the Cold War sharpened, so did the attacks on me, and in October 1947 we decided to leave Germany where I had been in charge of denazification of labor institutions and manpower allocation in the American Zone.

Our studies and work had convinced us that the future lay with some form of socialist organization of society, and since Czechoslovakia was then embarking on a democratic form of it, we decided to take our four children to Prague and find out what it was like before returning home. My wife worked in the Ministry of Culture and I lectured in economics, and did free-lance writing until 1954 when I was fortunate in receiving an appointment to the newly formed Economic Institute of the Czechoslovak Academy of Sciences. In 1962 I was elected a Corresponding Member of the Academy—one of three economists to have been so honored. In May 1968 I was awarded the Palacky Silver Medal for the promotion of Social Sciences by the Academy.

The August 1968 invasion came as a shock to us. I had spent the previous weekend explaining to an Australian friend the many economic, political, and moral reasons why I thought that there would be no intervention. I did warn him that I had made a similar analysis of the reasons why Japan would not attack the United States just four weeks before Pearl Harbor—and I still think that they were good, but obviously not compelling reasons.

After the tanks came the Czechoslovak people gave a fantastic display of peaceful resistance and of support for their government and its policies—but this I think it best to leave for poets to relate. Despite the lip service of the interveners to the ideas of the "Action Program," the reform was shot down in mid-flight. Within a short time almost every important leader was removed from office. In our Economic Institute all of the best economists (except for a few in special categories) were fired—and when my contract was renewed for four years (until 1974) I began to wonder what was wrong with me. When I finished writing this manuscript no one still at the Institute dared to read it, although others were enthusiastic about it. Censorship has been clamped down again, more drastic than any before. The Institute can no longer get basic materials needed for research. No serious criticism is possible. I began to look for lectures or some temporary position in the United States and, providentially, a teaching position opened up at Washington State University. During 1971-72 the political situation in Czechoslovakia deteriorated seriously, and now it appears that there will be no hope of useful economic research until, for some reason, the Russians leave.

During the more than 23 years that we lived in Prague and enjoyed the hospitality of the Czech and Slovak people we continued to study intensively the development of socialism and capitalism. Now, after long and serious consideration, I have decided that I am obligated to publish my conclusions from our study and experience in Czechoslovakia. Admittedly, this is a form of conceit. My excuse is that not many persons with "Western" economic training have had this experience. It is realized that this cannot be a definitive statement of the many problems, but it is hoped that it will be a positive addition to the persistent scientific discussion of the ways to attain a socialism that will be both efficient and humane.

GEORGE SHAW WHEELER

CHAPTER 1

The Inevitability of Change

Let us begin with the commonplace, since it is often the failure to recognize and understand the importance of ordinary things that results in misunderstanding. Change is inevitable. This applies to our entire environment, despite the seeming stability of many factors. It applies with particular force to the socioeconomic problems with which we are here immediately concerned, the situation in Czechoslovakia. All of us know this, yet some of the most learned of the many who have written about this small country have neglected to consider the effects of changes that have taken place in the last generation or even century, changes which are going on now and, in one form or another, in a good direction or bad, will continue to go on.

Man has an ambivalent attitude toward change: we like to travel—and then become homesick; we honor explorers—yet we expect our children to follow in our footsteps; we revere intellectual innovators such as Einstein—yet ignore their most profound thoughts on human relations. We even consider it a praiseworthy advance if we do not burn innovators at the stake—and in not a few countries even this modicum of security is largely reserved for the natural scientists, particularly for those who develop more efficient ways of destroying the human race. No such acceptance has been the lot of the real innovators in social relations, since their ideas almost inevitably disturb the positions of those in power. The intolerance of social innovation is phenomenal and is the root of much human suffering. It may be a resistance which protects an economic position, as the clinging to the system of latifundia in many parts of Latin America. But it may also involve other factors, such as the organized opposition to birth control. It may be based on a stubborn clinging to what is familiar, such as tastes in food. And it even may be just a bullheaded refusal to understand economic class advantages, such as the long opposition of the hierarchy of the American Federation of Labor to various forms of social security.

This resistance to change takes the form of defense of the *status quo* and often is intended to preserve certain institutions as well as the favored positions of the defenders. And in this there may be no small degree of success for a considerable period of time. But it is also most clear from history, and it is certainly even more true today in this era of rapid advances in science, that, in the long run, resistance to change is the most certain way of dooming an institution or a society. This is so patent that it hardly merits argument. It is not just that producers lose out if they fall behind in the use of more efficient technology (and, as Marx and Engels pointed out, control of this process of innovation is beyond the power of the capitalist). It is also that institutions and social policies must be adapted to changes in the mode of production. This also is at least partly beyond the control of man, and is the fundamental reason why capitalism must give way to higher forms of social organization.

The rate of change in the forces of production in most advanced societies is *at least* as high today as during the Industrial Revolution. It is in this light that we must regard the dialectics of change. In discussing dialectics Lenin quoted Engels:

> For it [dialectical philosophy] nothing is final, absolute or sacred. It reveals the transitory character of everything and in everything; nothing can endure before it except the uninterrupted process of becoming and passing away, of the endless ascendency from the lower to the higher.
> (F. Engels, *Ludwig Feuerbach,* English edition, 1946, p. 15. Lenin's quotation is from his article on Karl Marx in *Marx, Engels, Marxism,* Moscow, English edition, 1947, p. 23.)

This is the scientific Marxist outlook. A capitalist society, as Marx and Engels emphasized, has only limited and, in the end, inadequate, means of retarding change. A socialist society, particularly one with central planning and one which maintains all the controls of the "dictatorship of the proletariat," has much greater short-run powers to inhibit change. This becomes the greatest danger to the success of its economy, and ultimately to its security.

Economists and philosophers in Czechoslovakia have for some

time been pointing to this problem and its relation to the economic competition between capitalism and socialism.[1] One of the clearest statements of the interrelationships of science and technology to social development appears in the study by Radovan Richta and his group, *Civilization at the Crossroads*.[2] They have also related the general theories to specific Czechoslovak problems, such as the form of management of the economy. Science and technology, they argue, are developing "in the leading countries into a predominating dynamic force . . . and by the end of the century will create a new basis of civilization." (p. 31) They anticipate "a new cultural revolution created by technical progress and by general changes in the condition of human life." (p. 76)

Perhaps their most significant thesis is that this scientific-cultural revolution requires the Communist Party to reexamine the nature of its leading role. "The Communist Party," they wrote:

> can cope with this task only if it leaves the narrow scope of traditional power-political, administrative management and develops more advanced, more effective forms of social ("socio-political") management, a whole gamut of new approaches and forms aimed at creating technical, economic, sociological-psychological and anthropological conditions for *socialist creativeness,* and if it subordinates to them the hitherto existing instruments of management. (p. 148)

Most of the gains of capitalism in terms of increased output and increased productivity have come from innovation, from new technology and improved methods of production, not from extensive duplication of existing forms of capital. It is true that underdeveloped societies, particularly those with good natural resources and reserves of manpower, can make large advances in national product even if their investments are not in the most modern techniques. But in a developed economy, extensive investment is no substitute for dynamic innovation and the use of new technology as the prime source of increased productivity and growth. Most of us

---

[1] See George S. Wheeler, *Kapitalismus a automatizace*, (Capitalism Faces Automation), Academia, Prague, 1961, p. 360.

[2] Radovan Richta and others, *Civilizace na rozcestí: Společenské a lidské souvislosti vědeckotechnické revoluce* (Civilization at the Crossroads: Social and Human Implications of the Scientific and Technical Revolution), Svoboda, Prague, 1966.

do not realize how much our past increases in output and in consumer incomes have depended upon changes in technology and how little upon simple duplication of existing types of productive capacity. Robert M. Solow has calculated for the United States in the period 1909 to 1949 that output per man-hour doubled and that of this increase 87.5 percent was due to technical change and only 12.5 percent to increased amount of capital in use. (Solow, *The Review of Economics and Statistics,* August 1957, p. 320.)

We may well wonder at such precision in economics, but E. F. Denison later arrived at nearly identical figures: 85 percent of economic growth in the first half of the twentieth century in the United States was due to improved technology, including education. (Denison, *The Sources of Economic Growth in the United States,* 1962, p. 103.) More recently, and perhaps reflecting the current high rate of innovation, Simon Kuznets argued that the inescapable conclusion is that the direct contribution of man-hours and capital accumulation would hardly account for more than a tenth of the growth in per capita product—probably less. (Kuznets, *Modern Economic Growth,* 1966, p. 81.)

We conclude that if socialism is to surpass capitalism in this era of scientific advance, it must make sure that it has superior means of innovation, methods even more effective than the anarchic but ruthless pressures of capitalist competition. This means that socialist societies (and usually this means also the Communist Party in its leading role) must develop highly effective and specific ways of promoting new scientific thinking, for this is the basis for all advance. Since there can be no change or advance without risk, it means also that socialism must encourage risk-taking both in the area of technology of production and in working out satisfactory social policies. If a socialist society does not effectively motivate its administrators and managers to welcome changes that contribute to efficiency of production, to rising standards of living and to general cultural development, it will very soon find itself in serious trouble.

If a society permits stagnation, even *comparative* stagnation, it will, in this epoch of instantaneous communication, find its people increasingly alienated. And this process of alienation is more rapid and more complete in a society with a politically mature people using modern means of communication and travel. The more educated people are, the better informed they become, the less tolerant they are of both dictation and stagnation. A nation with such a people must take the lead in innovation if it is to prosper and endure.

CHAPTER 2

The Institutional Background

The area that is now Czechoslovakia lies at the crossroads of European trade routes and has repeatedly been invaded and occupied by foreign armies. During long periods of occupation the Czech and Slovak peoples have struggled to preserve their national existence, and these struggles have had a profound influence on their attitude toward national sovereignty and liberty. The political history of Czechoslovakia can be traced back to the Great Moravian Empire which reached the peak of its power between 870 and 894. But more enduring in its impact upon Czech society was the revolutionary Hussite movement that swept through Bohemia and Moravia after the Catholic hierarchy burnt Jan Hus at the stake in Constance in 1415. The Hussite movement was not only against the decadence of the Church but was equally against feudal oppression and exploitation.[1] It was the first broad movement for a classless, just social order, and one of the great forerunners of the Reformation in Europe.

Even more significant for our purposes of explaining the events in Czechoslovakia in 1968 were the struggles for independence culminating in victory and the formation of the Republic of Czechoslovakia in 1918. The brief history of the first Republic, with its alliance with France and Great Britain, culminating in the betrayal at Munich, followed by Nazi occupation and internal disruption, and finally the long struggle together during World War II for liberation from fascism, all helped to determine the political orientation of the people and the kind of socialism to which they aspire.

We do not propose to review this history, but only to point to the factors which are most significant. These are:

1) The existing forms of production and social relations;

---

[1] The Hussite movement was communist in form. One can still see today in Tabor, the Hussite stronghold, the great stone tubs in which each applicant was required to deposit his personal possessions before he could join the community.

The Institutional Background

2) The level of development of industry, agriculture, and service;
3) The stage of development of class structure;
4) Science, education, and culture;
5) Forms of planning and management, competition, monopoly and incentives; and,
6) Experience with revolution and democracy, struggle for sovereignty.

At the time of the formation of the Czechoslovak Republic the level of economic development of its Czech and Slovak nations was quite different. Slovakia had been under the hegemony of Hungary for roughly a thousand years and was mainly a land of small-scale private farms.[2] Its people, without schools in their own language, had stubbornly maintained their language and culture. They were strongly influenced by the Catholic religion. In contrast, industry in Bohemia and Moravia (the "Czech lands"), which had more than 10 million of a total population of 13.2 million, was more advanced than that of the ruling country, Austria. There were coal mines, steel mills and armament works, textile and shoe factories, and a variety of other light industries, such as porcelain, glass, and bijouterie.

There has been a long history of concern for education in the area that is now Czechoslovakia, dating back to the introduction of the alphabet in 863. The towering figure in world intellectual development, educator Jan Amos Comenius (1592–1670), was exiled for his religious, political, and national views in the Counter-Reformation after the Catholics (mainly Germans) won the Battle of White Mountain in 1620. Prague, with its Charles University now more than 600 years old, has long been one of the main centers of European culture. It was a deeply based culture, one struggling for development under conditions of foreign domination. Compulsory education was introduced in 1868–69. By the time of the defeat of the Monarchy 97 percent of the Czechs and 85 per-

---

[2] In 1918 only 12 percent of the industrial production of Czechoslovakia was in Slovakia. By 1967 about 22.4 percent of industrial production was Slovak (Bratislava *Pravda,* October 26, 1968). In 1930 nearly 57 percent of the population in Slovakia was dependent upon agriculture, while in the Czech lands only 25.5 percent was. (Czechoslovak State Statistical Office, *Statistická ročenka,* 1957, p. 43. Hereafter the *Statistická ročenka* will be referred to as the *Statistical Yearbook.*)

cent of the Slovaks were literate, and practically all adults were interested in politics.

The 1920 constitution of the new Republic of Czechoslovakia was one of the most advanced in the world in its parliamentary form and in guarantees of legal and civil rights to its citizens. This reflected the long struggles for national liberation and the humanitarian thinking of such men as Thomas G. Masaryk, but it was also the result of an attempt to offset the appeal of socialism to the workers. An objective proof of the extent of that appeal is the fact that in the first elections the Social Democratic Party (before its 1921 split with the Communists) polled 25 percent of the total vote. By the time of the 1925 election the fragmentation of parties was so great that 36 parties were competing for votes! The Communist Party was the second in size, with 943,000 votes and 41 deputies out of 300 in the House of Parliament.[3]

The economy of the new republic had difficulty in adjusting to its independent position outside the Austro-Hungarian monarchy and only regained the 1913 level of industrial output in 1928. Then came the world economic crisis of 1929 and in the depth of the following depression, in the spring of 1933, 920,000 workers were officially counted as unemployed—a catastrophic level in a country with only about 14 million inhabitants.[4] Out of this situation came an intensified class struggle, but with the working class badly fragmented by a narrow sectarianism. In the 1935 election the fascist Sudeten Germany Party received the most votes in Czechoslovakia, with 1,249,500 ballots—in Bohemia, 21.5 percent of the total. The Czechoslovak Social Democrats got 1,034,774 votes and the Communists 849,509 or 10.3 percent of the total. (*Statistical Yearbook*, 1937, p. 269.)

After the Munich betrayal had demonstrated the failure of a Western-oriented alliance to protect Czechoslovak sovereignty, many people looked for security in a Soviet alliance. The Nazi occupation, and liberation mainly at the hands of the socialist Soviet

---

[3] *Hospodářství ČSR na jaře 1946* (Czechoslovak Economy in the Spring of 1946), Svoboda, Prague, p. 11.

[4] *Facts About Czechoslovakia*, Orbis, 1958, p. 12. This total did not include hundreds of thousands of young people who never had a job and so were not registered or counted as unemployed or the other unemployed not on the rolls of the employment office. Josef Flek, who made a careful study of the situation, concluded that the real total of unemployed was at least 1,200,000.

Union, resulted in the majority of the people—not just the workers—turning to socialism. At the same time there was warm feeling for and often (because of the many immigrants to the United States) close family ties with the American people and an admiration for some of its political institutions. The political parties that had actively resisted the Nazis met in Košice, Slovakia, in April 1945 and agreed on a program oriented toward socialism and which provided for the nationalization of the banks and the key industries including those producing raw materials, and on the confiscation of the property of war criminals and those who had collaborated with the enemy.

A National Front government was formed with Eduard Beneš as president and Zdeněk Fierlinger (Social Democrat) as premier.[5] After the final victory this coalition government quickly carried out the nationalization of large enterprises and expelled from Czechoslovakia most persons who had elected (after Hitler came to power) to maintain their German nationality. By July 1947 only 20 percent of the industrial workers were employed in private industry. (Josef Goldmann, Josef Flek, and others, *Planned Economy in Czechoslovakia,* Orbis, 1949, p. 28.)

In the elections to Parliament in May 1946, conducted with a free choice of parties and by secret ballot, the Communist Party won 38 percent of the ballots cast. Together with the 13 percent won by the Social Democratic Party (with which it merged in 1948), the advocates of a fully socialist program had won an absolute majority in Parliament. President Beneš, according to the Constitution, called upon Klement Gottwald (Communist) to act as premier and form a new government. In this Cabinet the Communists held nine of the 26 posts, but these included the key positions of the Ministries of Interior (police), Foreign Affairs, Agriculture, Foreign Trade, and Information. The government drew up the First Two-Year Plan of Economic Reconstruction (1947–48), which was not a fully centralized model and tried to use market incentives as well as pricing and financial controls rather than admin-

---

[5] In general, in the formation of the government and local councils, and even in the management of the nationalized enterprises, the principle of parity was observed. This meant that each of the four parties in the Czech area got approximately 25 percent of the positions, and in the Slovak area each got half. For a time there were *four* directors of some enterprises! In the courts, too, the principle of parity was observed—even after the 1946 election in cases dealing with war criminals.

istrative directives. There was also nominal control of investments. We say "nominal" because there was a large "black market" in both materials and in consumer goods. A large part of the investment, particularly in housing and in private industry, was outside of the plan. In fact, as Goldmann and Flek pointed out, more houses were built illegally in some areas than legally under the Two-Year Plan. There was a persistent tendency to favor private investment not only in housing but, more seriously, in industry. This "continued misplacement of investment" hampered the nationalized sector (about four-fifths of the total) of the economy and threatened the success of the Plan. (Josef Goldmann, Josef Flek, and others, *Planned Economy in Czechoslovaki,* Orbis, Prague, 1949 pp. 24 and 43–45.)

The response to this by those who favored a full development of socialism and planning was to push for further nationalization of the remaining private industry. A tension developed with those who favored the return to private industry and the formation as in France and Italy of a coalition government without the Communists. With active United States support, this was no idle threat. This crisis was resolved in February 1948 by a victory of the socialist forces which eliminated the right-wing ministers from the cabinet. The change was bloodless and completely in accordance with the Constitution of 1920, but the decisive factor was the show of power of the working people through demonstrations of the trade unions, token strikes, and later through displays of the armed workers' militia.[6] With the changes of the "February Events" the socialist revolution (which might be said to have started in 1944 with the Slovak Uprising) was completed, with the working class fully in control of the state power.

"Dictatorship of the Proletariat"

The consolidation of working-class state power by the February events also ultimately determined the general model of central-

---

[6] As one who witnessed these events I can testify that the power shown by the workers was indeed persuasive. It was quite understandable that President Beneš accepted the resignation of the minority of the ministers and instructed Klement Gottwald to form a new government. The newly formed, armed People's Militia stayed in the background until after Beneš approved the cabinet change.

The Institutional Background 11

ized planning and administration of the economy, although the first draft of the First Five-Year Plan was still far from the Soviet model. That came only in 1950 and 1951 as the Cold War brought an abrupt revision of the "peacetime" model, a shift to heavy industry, and the substitution of dictatorial for economic and democratic forms of management.[7] (See Josef Flek and Josef Goldmann, "O dvouletce a první pětiletce," *Příspěvky k d ějinám KSČ*, No. 3, 1965, pp. 428–32.)

Politically, a period of the "dictatorship of the proletariat" was inaugurated in February 1948 with the purpose of eliminating all influence of the capitalist class and any possibility of the return to capitalism. In May 1948 a new Constitution was adopted which stressed the "progressive and humanitarian traditions in our history" and spelled out in considerable detail *economic* rights, such as equal pay for equal work for men and women, and the right (and duty) to work. These economic rights, which corrected the more serious inequalities that existed under the First Republic, were further elaborated in the Constitution of July 11, 1960. The development of these economic and social rights marked a fundamental advance in the life of the working people. In some of them, such as the availability of education, free medical care, and maternity leave, Czechoslovakia has come to hold a leading position in the world.

At this point, however, we must return to the methods of management and control of the economy. This is a question of political power, and here a study of the Constitutions reveals some significant information. A written constitution is not only a summary of a nation's political hopes and doctrines—it is also, presumably, a statement of the allocation of state power. The opening "Declaration" of the 1960 Constitution states: "Socialism has triumphed in our country! We have entered a new stage in our history, and we are determined to go forward to new and still higher goals."[8]

---

[7] In February 1950 the Central Committee of the Communist Party of Czechoslovakia decided to shift the Plan toward heavy industry and mining. Repeated changes followed, so that by March 1951 the plan for heavy engineering was nearly 50 percent above and the plan for mining 2.7 times that of the original plan. Employment expanded 18% in 1950. Note that these were *Party,* not government, decisions. (*Plánované hospodářství* January 1951, and *Nová mysl,* No. 8–9, 1950, pp. 663–64, and No. 3, March 1951, p. 177.)

[8] These quotations, here and below, are from the official English translation published by Orbis, Prague, in 1960.

Article 2 states:

1) All power in the Czechoslovak Socialist Republic shall belong to the working people.
2) The working people shall exercise state power through representative bodies which are elected by them, controlled by them, and accountable to them.
3) Representative bodies of the working people in the Czechoslovak Socialist Republic shall be: the National Assembly (Parliament), the Slovak National Council, and national committees. The authority of other state organs shall be derived from them.

This clearly makes the National Assembly the supreme power of the state. Neither the May 9, 1948, nor the 1960 Constitution mentions the dictatorship of the proletariat. On the contrary, the Declaration of the 1960 Constitution states flatly:

> There are no longer any exploiting classes, exploitation of man by man has been eliminated forever. In our country all of the main problems of the transition from capitalist to socialist society have already been solved. (pp. 43–44)

Section III of the Declaration begins:

> All our efforts are now directed at creating the material and moral conditions for the transition of our society to communism. While developing socialist statehood we shall perfect our socialist democracy by increasing the direct participation of the working people in the administration of the State and in the management of the economy, consolidating the political and moral unity of our society, safeguarding the defense of our country, cherishing the revolutionary achievements of the people and providing conditions for the development of all their creative abilities. (p. 44)

Since the dictatorship of the proletariat has only one purpose, the abolition of the power of the capitalist class, this statement means that by 1960 it had fulfilled its mission in the Č.S.S.R. as far as the *internal* class struggle was concerned. External defenses are a different matter, but interal repressions *after* classes have been eliminated weaken those defenses and seriously retard the growth of the world socialist movement. The Declaration is an indication of the fundamental desire of the Czechoslovak people to perfect their democracy by direct participation rather than by a continuation of rigid internal controls—controls exercised by a bureaucracy not responsible or accountable to the National Assembly. If we are to understand the nature of these controls, their advantages and disadvantages, we must begin with the role of the Communist Party. The May 1948 Constitution does not mention the Communist Party. The Constitution of 1960, however, refers to the leading role of the Communist Party not only in the Declaration but also in Articles 4 and 6 which read:

> The guiding force in society and in the State is the vanguard of the working class, the Communist Party of Czechoslovakia, a voluntary militant alliance of the most active and most politically conscious citizens from the ranks of the workers, farmers and intelligentsia.

Article 6 reads:

> The National Front of Czechs and Slovaks, in which the people's organizations are associated, is the political expression of the alliance of the working people of town and country, led by the Communist Party of Czechoslovakia.

These are the only references to the powers and the duties of the Communist Party, and they are both vague and in at least partial contradction to the assignment of supreme powers to the National Assembly. How did it come about, then, that from February 1948 on the Communist Party in fact exercised a decisive and pervasive power not only in political affairs but in the management of the economy and in every phase of social life? We will not find the answer to this in the Constitution, but in the actual revolutionary situation and in the dominance of Stalinist concepts. Stalin wrote:

> The dictatorship of the proletariat is in essence the "dictatorship" of its vanguard, the "dictatorship" of its Party as the force which guides the proletariat.
> (Joseph Stalin, *Problems of Leninism,* Moscow, 1940, p. 135.)

This formulation in practice meant a wide departure from Lenin's concept of "All Power to the Soviets," which were *elected* bodies. It meant that, from the start, as the eastern part of Czechoslovak territory was being liberated in 1945, the Communist Party began to organize its own base of power. The "People's Militia," organized in February 1948, was an armed force independent of the army and police, composed of Communist Party members (men and women) mainly in the factories, but not including all workers. It was organized as a *reserve* of Party power. It was accountable only to and was under the direction of the Party leadership. The Militia undoubtedly had the approval of the majority of the workers, and this was its ultimate sanction, but it was an instrument of the Party which did not require that approval to be put to any parliamentary test.

The People's Militia was, as we have seen, important in the 1948 crisis, but it was only one source of the power of the Communist Party. In the routine operation of the economy other factors soon became of much greater importance. Most important was the control of positions of power throughout the administrative apparatus. This process, too, began as the Soviet armies, and the Slovaks and Czechs fighting with it, freed the eastern part of the country from the Nazi occupiers. Under Communist leadership people's courts and local committees were set up which took over factories and tried collaborators. Later, when the Ministry of Interior came under the control of the Communist Party, the police began to play an increasing role in power politics. Many opponents of the Communists, such as Edward Táborský who had been personal aide to President Beneš, regarded these tactics as unfair.[9] But they were the natural and inevitable result of the policy of delaying as long as possible the opening of the Second Front. This left the Soviet Union with the main task and the enormous cost of defeating the Nazis. The prestige of the Soviet Union in the areas they freed was correspondingly great.

Also it was inevitable that many people, and not just the Communist leaders, would turn to the Soviet Union as their model, look

---

[9] See Edward Táborský's bitter book, *Communism in Czechoslovakia, 1948–1960,* Princeton, 1961, pp. 13–15. Not a little of what Táborský wrote is true, but it is so one-sided that it can not be independently relied upon.

The Institutional Background

to it for continued protection, seek and accept its advice. Strong elements of this gratitude and friendship remained even after doubts later began to grow about the continued usefulness of the old Stalin economic and political model in Czechoslovakia. Stalin, of course, was not content with a voluntary relationship as advisor. This became clear on more than one occasion as, for example, when on July 4, 1947, Czechoslovakia voted to accept the invitation to discuss "Marshall Plan" aid. Stalin immediately summoned Gottwald and other government leaders to Moscow, thoroughly berated them, and forced them to agree to a reversal of the policy. This humiliation was a particularly serious blow to Gottwald's prestige and it served to bring home again to all government leaders the extreme difficulty that Czechoslovakia, as a small country, would have in maintaining an independent foreign and internal economic policy.

It must be remembered that these events were taking place in a period of sharply intensified Cold War. Even before February 1948 the United States was discriminating against Czechoslovak trade. John Foster Dulles, Wall Street lawyer and at that time the most influential man in shaping United States foreign policy, told the Senate Foreign Relations Committee shortly before the February 1948 revolution:

I think the Potsdam agreement, for all intents and purposes, should now be treated as pretty much of a dead letter. (U. S. Senate, Committee on Foreign Relations, *Hearings on the European Recovery Program,* Government Printing Office, January 1948, p. 612.)

Germany was one of the sore spots in the developing Cold War and both the Czechoslovaks and the Russians were, for obvious reasons, acutely allergic to the United States policy of restoring monopoly capitalism in the Western (now Bonn) part. This was another reason why many Czechoslovaks felt that strengthening socialism, even at the cost of dictatorial methods, was fully justified. It seemed that a third world war was in preparation. Rearmament was under way, with the real danger that atomic weapons would be used against socialism. Fear, even hysteria, was the order of the day, with a young man, Richard Nixon, starting his political career on the basis of a Communist witch-hunt. The Dulles brothers and the notorious Senator Joseph McCarthy were riding high. It was not a time when legal provisions for protection of the politically accused were given much weight, and arbitrary measures were approved because it was thought that they were emergency measures. It was in this setting that central planning began in Czechoslovakia, a revolutionary setting and one in which the worldwide class struggle was in an acute and only partly rational stage. It should also be recalled that rationing was still necessary, and this also tended to perpetuate the wartime centralization of administration of the economy.

Central Planning

In one of the few passages in which Marx or Engels wrote about planning, Engels emphasized the key importance of the social ownership of the means of production to planning and, in turn, the importance of planning to social development. In an almost poetic passage Engels wrote:

> The seizure of the means of production by society puts an end to commodity production, and therewith to the domination of the product over the producer. Anarchy in social production is replaced by conscious organization on a planned basis. The struggle for individual existence comes to an end. And at this point man in a certain sense finally separates from the animal world. The objective and extraneous forces which have hitherto dominated history will then pass under the control of men themselves. It is only from this point onward that men with full consciousness will shape their own history. It is humanity's leap from the realm of necessity into the realm of freedom. . . . A social production upon a predetermined plan now becomes possible. (Engels, *Anti-Dühring,* English edition, Moscow, 1947, pp. 420–21 and 423.)

Here is the dialectical concept of the use of the greater controls of social planning to attain a "realm of freedom." We shall return briefly to the question of commodity production and the market, since these comments by Engels greatly influenced the thinking of many later economists. Here we wish to point to the high hopes that Marxist economists held for planning, and that it was with great eagerness, even with a sense of euphoria, that they greeted the nationalization of industry and the opportunity, and necessity, to embark upon social planning.

The revolutionary political situation in Czechoslovakia in 1945–48, with its sharp class struggle and the need for economic recovery, required central planning, since the plan was the instrument for controlling the entire development and orientation of the socialist sector of the economy. It must be remembered also that only a centralized model of managing a socialist economy had ever succeeded, and the Soviet model had performed in a manner which had confounded all of its critics. It was quite natural that some features of that economic model, the abolition of private ownership of the basic means of production and the centrally planned allocation of production resources (including labor power), would be incorporated in the model for the management of the Czechoslovak economy.

Yet it must not be thought that the Czechoslovaks were so naïve as to take the Soviet model without thinking that some modification for the special Czechoslovak conditions might be desirable or that from the first theirs was only a copy of the Soviet administrative model. In fact the leading economists strongly favored an experimental attitude in the use of financial and economic controls. This can best be seen by quoting from publications of that period:

> Czechoslovakia occupies a special place among the countries that have adopted the principle of a planned economy. In most of these the nationalization of large-scale industrial enterprise and of banking, and the development of economic planning, is taking place under quite different conditions from those prevailing here. In the new democracies of eastern and southeastern Europe agriculture dominates the economy, productive capacity is little developed, and the standard of living is comparatively low. The real large-scale industrialization of Russia did not begin until after the October Revolution. Czechoslovakia, on the other hand, presents a different and individual picture. In industrial production—both in terms of total volume and of output per head of population—Czechoslovakia ranks among the ten most important industrial states in the world: here, for the first time in history, is a country with a predominantly industrial

economy, with a relatively high standard of living, which has socialized, if not all, at least the greater and decisive portion of the means of production. . . .
The systematic collection and collation of material gleaned from the Czechoslovak economy is the more essential because here —though we may but rarely realize this—something entirely new is being created.
(Goldmann and others, *op.cit.*, pp. 15–17.)

Such an experimental and scientific attitude was not appreciated by those who held the decisive political power. Furthermore the First Five-Year Plan was oriented toward peacetime production, not the development of heavy war industries. Then the Cold War and the Stalinists took over and within two years after the above was written (in 1948) a policy of systematic removal of economists and others with democratically innovative ideas was adopted. Dr. Ludvík Frejka, then head of the President's Economic Office, one of the chief framers of the Two-Year Plan and First Five-Year Plan, and writer of the introduction to the above-quoted study, was executed as a result of the Slánský trials. Dr. Josef Goldmann, then Director of the Institute of Economic and Social Research in Prague, spent five years in prison and then five more years as a factory laborer. Others, such as Pavel Eisler, were somewhat more fortunate, working in factories and farms. But the economy of Czechoslovakia suffered a severe loss not only because the false charges of counterrevolution, Zionism, conspiracy, and sabotage deprived the country of the direct services of many of its best and most devoted scientists, but also because the trials and prosecutions of these leaders intimidated all others who were managing the economy. A high premium had been placed upon conformity and mediocrity just when Czechoslovak planning was getting under way.

The First Two-Year Plan in Czechoslovakia was demanding in its high targets for recovery, but it was necessarily a recovery plan and not a full or typical central plan. Nevertheless its description, given by Dr. Goldmann, one of the economists active both in formulating and administering it, is a useful introduction to planning methods:

The Two-Year Plan is essentially a set of production targets, mutually correlated and coordinated by a number of "material

The Institutional Background

balances," i.e., balances of raw materials, coal, man-power, etc. Productivity of labor, costing, marketing, finance, etc., are not, and could not have been, part of the Plan in that detailed and scientifically elaborated way in which they form part of a Soviet Five-Year Plan. Some general targets have been set for labor productivity, such as an increase in average output per head to 110 percent of the prewar level and specific figures have been given in some cases. Production was, of course, related to prospective needs in each single case. Price problems were examined, if only incidentally. On the whole, however, these aspects of the economy are not yet being planned according to an interrelated, balanced, and all-embracing plan.

The sectional plans for the various industries were worked out by the appropriate Central Directorates for nationalized firms and, as far as private firms are concerned, by the Industrial Associations of that branch of industry. Coordination of the sectional plans and uniform planning technique were secured through the work of the planning department of the Ministry of Industry and, at a higher level, of the State Planning Office and the Central Planning Commission. In this body the parties of the National Front are represented by their economic experts. The Central Planning Commission, being at the same time an expert and a political body, combined general supervision and direction of the elaboration of the Plan with the important political function of facilitating, through common work on the Plan, its final acceptance by all parties of the National Front.

(Goldmann, *Czechoslovakia: Test Case of Nationalization*, Orbis, Prague, 1947, p. 36.)

It can be seen that from the beginning Czechoslovak planning had its complications. But central planning of resource allocation and investment also has tremendous advantages over the unplanned market economy in that it permits a society to mobilize its resources to attain specific goals. Both existing productive facilities and new investments can be controlled and channeled to specific purposes; for example, this is always done when equipping armies during wars. Central planners can determine not only the direction of investment, but also have a good deal of control over the proportion of the national income that goes to investment and to consumption.

Not only is central planning advantageous in control of the amount of resources used for various purposes, it also *has the opportunity* of using resources more *efficiently* because it can avoid the duplication of investments and idle resources that characterize an economy relying upon market forces to determine resource allocation. When the central planning model was adopted in Czechoslovakia, the bitter experiences with wasted resources, particularly mass unemployment of the prewar period, were fresh in the minds of all policy makers. For many economists who lived through these experiences, the greater efficiency of socialist planning in the use of resources appeared to be a decisive advantage.

Theoretical concepts, such as the above-quoted statement of Engels that "the seizure of the means of production by society puts an end to commodity production," played a big (but not exclusive) role in determining the actual policies and the forms of planning and management adopted in the Soviet Union and later applied in Czechoslovakia. Professor Ota Šik has thoroughly examined this impact of theory upon actual economic developments, and we need not review it here.[10]

We are concerned with the fact that the theoretical statements denigrating the market were allowed to become dogma ruling out experimentation. This was quite alien to Lenin's attitude toward these theoretical ideas. In defending the partial reintroduction of market relationships after attempts at eliminating commodity relations Lenin said:

> Borne along on the crest of the wave of enthusiasm, rousing first the political enthusiasm and then the military enthusiasm of the people, we reckoned that by directly relying on this enthusiasm we would be able to accomplish economic tasks just as great as the political and military tasks we accomplished. We reckoned —or perhaps it would be truer to say that we presumed without reckoning adequately—on being able to organize the state pro-

---

[10] Ota Šik, *Plan and Market under Socialism,* Academia, Prague, 1967, edition in English, especially Part I, "Development of a Socialist Market Theory and Its Application in Czechoslovakia." Ota Šik, born in 1919 in Pilsen, was interned by the Nazis in Mauthausen concentration camp from 1942 to 1945. He was the leading economist in Czechoslovakia, a Member of the Academy of Sciences, a member of the Central Committee of the Communist Party, and from April to August 21, 1968, a Deputy Premier of the Czechoslovak Government. After the invasion he became an exile teaching at the University of Basel, Switzerland.

duction and the state distribution of products on Communist lines in a small-peasant country directly by an order of the proletarian state. Experience has proved that we were wrong.
(V. I. Lenin, "Fourth Anniversary of October Revolution," *Selected Works,* II, Part 2, Foreign Languages Publishing House, Moscow, 1952, p. 601.)

This is the scientific attitude: to test a theory that seems to be reasonable, and if it proves wrong to admit error and to change the policy—and the theory. Note well that Lenin said *"We* were wrong"—not "they" were wrong. The later replacement of this attitude by one which pretended to omniscience and infallibility, relied on precedent, feared change and tried to avoid all risks, became a solid block to the understanding and solution of many practical problems. We must try to find the causes for this degeneration into bureaucratic dogmatism because it appears to be a tendency not confined to one era or country, or to the traits of one man, but to be inherent in varying degree in all societies. We shall try to demonstrate by the Czechoslovak example that a society whose theories and institutions tend to foster dogmatic attitudes will have extreme difficulty in promoting science and in adapting new technologies for its economic use. A society which fails in these respects may continue to *exist* for some time but it cannot successfully compete in the modern world.

Administrative Price Setting

Theory and lack of experience combined to make it seem that central fixing of prices in an economy would not be difficult. Indeed, price policy appeared to be a highly useful instrument of general social policy. Medical care and education could be free, the prices of other things, such as housing and bread, could be subsidized. Other commodities could be sold at their actual costs, while some products, such as hard liquor and cigarettes, could be heavily taxed to support other worthy social activities. In short, prices, freed from market determination, could become an instrument for encouraging socially useful trends and for discouraging those regarded as undesirable. For the social reformers this was an attractive prospect and one that could be defended on humanitarian grounds.

One of the pioneers in considering the relationship between planning and price fixing was the Polish economist, Oscar Lange, who as early as 1938 published a polemic against those who, like Mises, Hayek, and Robbins, argued that socialist economies could not establish a rational system of prices. (O. Lange and F. W. Taylor, *On the Economic Theory of Socialism,* Minneapolis, 1938.) Lange, assuming a decentralized model with a quasi market, proposed a system of successive approximations which would result in workable "accounting prices." Many years later, after the development of electronic computers, he still pointed to the usefulness of this method—and many economists are now arguing the advantage of "accounting" or "shadow prices" *together with* some form of market, in centrally setting at least part of the prices of a planned economy. (See further, Essays in Honor of Oscar Lange, *On Political Economy and Econometrics,* Warsaw, 1964.) We do not intend at all to belittle the contribution made by Oscar Lange when we say that at first he underestimated the complexity of central price setting, and along with others, thought that it would be comparatively simple.[11] This is essentially a static concept of pricing and therefore is difficult to use in a dynamic economy. In fact the setting, or freezing, of prices *is* deceptively easy. But, once set, those inflexible prices (that cannot reflect socially necessary costs) lead to difficulties that are unforeseeable and weird in their complexities. But this we can see best by the actual Czechoslovak experiences to which we shall return in Chapter 5.

In emergencies all countries, capitalist and socialist, ration or allocate both consumer goods and materials of production. Usually the market is allowed to continue to function in a limited way and for less essential and more available commodities. This is necessary in the case of consumer goods to maintain some equality in distribution, and to protect consumers from black-market price rises. Allocation of raw materials and semifinished products (and even of producers' equipment) is done not only in order to assure the production of essential goods, but also in the name of efficiency. Such replacement of the market in the allocation of

---

[11] In 1938 Lange wrote in regard to central price fixing: "The technique of attaining this end is very simple; the central planning board has to fix prices and see to it that all managers of plants, industries and resources do their accounting on the basis of the prices fixed by the central planning board." (Oscar Lange, *On the Economic Theory of Socialism,* McGraw-Hill edition, 1964, p. 81.)

The Institutional Background

commodities can work fairly well for a limited time and for a limited number of goods.

In the case of both consumer and producer goods, however, rationing and allocation generate all kinds of problems: problems of amount and quality of the commodities, of their prices, the justice of subjectively made decisions, administrative costs, speed of decision, etc. That is why nearly all advanced countries abandon the rationing of goods as soon as the ending of the emergency permits. But the socialist countries have generally operated on a centralized model which includes the allocation of the main raw materials and many forms of semifinished products. For this reason some of the same factors which beset the wartime rationing of producers' goods also plague the planned economies. In some cases these problems can be brought under control. In others the difficulties accumulate and spread to other sectors of the economy despite the most strenuous and elaborate efforts of control.

In the absence of market controls, the general tendency is to elaborate the administrative controls. In place of competitive pressures or profit incentives were substituted the norms of the plan. These norms were set by the central planning office on the assumption that output would increase for the economy by about six percent annually—a not unreasonable assumption. But in applying these growth targets the center had no way of knowing specifically what the real possibilities were for actual operations of the plants. Those in which technology was stagnant had to impose a speedup on their workers, or increase their numbers to meet the target. Those in which there was rapid technological advance had an easy time, and further relieved the pressure by concealing as much as possible of their technical advance from the planning office. In this way they could be certain to fulfill the plan and receive their premiums.

The norms or targets were not self-enforcing and it required detailed reporting and much investigation even to be sure that the plan had been fulfilled, or to determine the extent of the failure—to say nothing of its cause. A multiplicity of control agencies grew up, not just because of Stalin's predilection for them, but because each agency—illustrating Parkinson's law—sought to expand its functions and powers. A flood of directives poured out from these agencies. In 1962 the Ministry of Agriculture alone was processing and issuing *each working day about 1,000 directives, circulars, in-*

structions, and other memoranda. (Rudé právo, April 17, 1962.) Just filing (or discarding) them took an excessive amount of time; reading them was a dreary task. Complying with them was often impossible because they were contradictory or because the reality at the production level was quite different from what it was believed to be by the various central agencies.

Because of the lack of information, and equally because it was physically impossible for the center to handle the multiplicity of problems which came to it, there was both a flood of directives and at the same time intolerable delays in obtaining answers to even simple questions. To the producing units, beset with problems and without power to resolve them, the increasing delays and increasing complexities of the centralized administration were both frustrating and alienating. Seemingly reasonable forms of management broke down, incentives failed to evoke responses. Instead of performing a liberating role as Engels had envisaged, the *overcentralized model* of planning turned into a maze—a trap restricting the freedom of workers and factory managers alike, killing initiative and bringing technological innovation almost to a standstill, and finally even reducing real wages.

Before we turn to a detailed examination of just how all this took place we must first show the initial successes of the centralized model—successes which other countries, in earlier stages of development and which still have unused manpower or unusually fine natural resources, can continue for a time to achieve with only partial modification of the early model. The long toleration of the centralized model can only be understood in the light of these successes, because no one, whether he has had experiences with democratic forms and methods or not, likes to be dictated to in the manner which became customary for the administrators of the centralized plan.

CHAPTER 3

Economic Growth

The introduction of socialist centralized planning into Czechoslovakia initiated a phase of growth which was then—in its scope and duration—practically without precedent for an advanced economy. Unlike some other economies which later had long periods of high growth rates, the developments in Czechoslovakia were based solely on its own internal resources.[1] This advance was the more remarkable, and at the time more satisfying, because it contrasted sharply with the experiences after World War I. Then it took until 1928 for industrial production to regain the 1913 level—a period of 10 years. With economic crises and another war (and one cannot brush those wars and crises aside as not a part of the capitalist system), *industrial production in September 1945 was only about one-half that of 1913!*[2] This was the heritage with which central planning began in Czechoslovakia in 1945—one which older workers remember to this day.

In contrast to this, the First Two-Year Plan (1947–48) succeeded not only in restoring the economy (with changes), but in surpassing the 1937 level of industrial output, by around 10 percent. Total private consumption advanced less, partly as a result of one of the most disastrous droughts in the history of Czechoslovak agriculture. As can be seen in Table 1, private consumption in terms of comparable values was higher in 1948 than in 1937, but still below the 1930 level. But with the big improvement in public consumption, total consumption in 1948 was well ahead of prewar

---

[1] Through many devices to stimulate investment and consumption some (but not all) capitalist countries have maintained much higher rates of growth of gross national product than before World War II. Much can be learned from a study of the reasons for this, particularly in the use of science and new technology. But note also that at least in the case of West Germany and Japan, part of the initial impulse for their growth rate came from large-scale investments by the United States which permitted the equipping of new plant capacity with the latest technology.

[2] See Goldmann, *Test Case of Nationalization,* p. 14, and Karel Král, *Working People in Czechoslovakia,* Práce, Prague, 1953, p. 16.)

(line 7). Gross national product, at 86.1 thousand million crowns, was also greater than in either the prewar years—years, incidentally, which were much above the average.[3]

TABLE 1. Czechoslovak Gross National Expenditure for Consumption and Investment in 1937 prices (thousand million crowns)

	1930	1937	1948	1966
1. Private consumption	61.0	57.5	58.1	120.1
2. food		27.0	26.9	51.3
3. housing		6.9	6.4	17.0
4. other products		23.6	24.8	35.3
5. other services				16.5
6. Public consumption[a]	9.3	13.7	15.9	50.0
7. Total	70.3	71.2	74.0	170.1
8. Gross investment	14.2	14.5	9.9	56.6
9. buildings	6.7	5.7	5.7	25.7
10. Other (in machines and equipment)	7.5	8.8	4.2	30.9
11. Resources used, total	84.5	85.7	83.9	226.7
12. Other[b]	0.5	−1.0	2.2	13.9
13. Gross National Product	85.0	84.7	86.1	240.6

[a] Education, scientific research and development, transport, post, medical service, social care, culture (subsidized theaters, music, sports, etc.), administration.

[b] Balance of foreign trade (goods and services), changes in inventories, in 1966; also losses (which before 1966 were included in the changes of inventories).

Source: Based on Jaroslav Krejčí, "The Development of Czechoslovak Economy in Global Analysis," *Politická ekonomie* No. 6/1968, pp. 581–597. Krejčí used official statistics as the basis for his calculations.

We choose this table which emphasizes consumption because total public and private consumption, not *inputs* into the economy, is the real test of its success. And by this test the planned economy in Czechoslovakia was incomparably more successful than the capitalism which it replaced. After the initial success in restoring the economy by 1948, it continued to advance sharply (although not smoothly) so that by 1966 total consumption (in 1937 prices) had reached more than 170 thousand million crowns. It should be

---

[3] Note the surprisingly high ratio of investment to gross national product in 1930 of 23 percent. In 1948 about 17 percent was invested, and even in 1966 less than a fifth of the gross product was invested. In 1937 a large part of the investment went into improving the defense fortifications.

borne in mind that the per capita increase in consumption as compared with prewar was relatively greater than the increase in total consumption because the 1969 population was roughly 3.5 percent below that of 1937, both as the result of war losses and because nearly three million Germans fled or were expelled—many of whom were highly productive workers.[4] The loss of these workers was one reason why many persons regarded the. First Five-Year Plan, which set the goal of doubling the 1948 level of industrial production in only five years, as too ambitious. Even the planners had their misgivings, yet the original plan was overfulfilled (102 percent). (*Facts about Czechoslovakia,* Orbis, 1958, p. 20.)

During the First Republic there had been an erosion of real wages of employed workers, declining from an average of 547 crowns per month for insured workers in 1920 to only 445 crowns in 1937. Socialism reversed this trend, with real wages rising from 2,663 crowns in 1946 to 5,216 crowns monthly in 1952, or about double. Here we compare only *trends* since the inflation of the war prevents comparability of these figures. (Karel Král, *Working People in Czechoslovakia,* Práce, Prague, 1953, p. 20.)

However, the fact that a drastic monetary reform became necessary in 1953 indicates that a serious disproportion had already developed between heavy industry and industries producing consumer goods. In that reform many workers lost all their savings. For example, our neighbors who had been saving to buy furniture lost all but a nominal amount of it. This experience should have given pause to those who insisted that "planned proportional development is a fundamental law of socialism." It is a commentary on the situation in economic science that the phrase continued to be repeated despite such experiences.[5]

Even so, the Plans could not have been fulfilled and the high rate of growth of national product could not have been reached if the Plans had not effectively mobilized the resources of the country. In fact, a remarkable level of enthusiasm was generated, with

---

[4] In 1937 about 425,000 Germans were employed in industry alone. By December 1946 there were only 61,000. (Goldmann, *Test Case,* p. 23.)

[5] As recently as December 1971 we find Soviet economist L. Leontyev arguing: "It is the public ownership of the means of production and, consequently, of its results that serves as the foundation underlying the operation of the law governing planned, proportional development of the national economy—an objective economic law of socialism." (*Trud,* December 24, 1971.)

the people responding to both moral and material incentives. By 1952 about 60 percent of the workers were participating in socialist emulation. In the period 1948–52 over 200,000 suggestions for improving efficiency or quality had been turned in by the workers and accepted for use. One reason for this enthusiasm was that the workers and the trade unions felt that they had a part in both shaping the original plan and in controlling its development. They participated in the management councils of the enterprises[6] (electing a third of the members) and had control of safety in the plants, administered the social insurance, and had much-improved recreational and vacation facilities. (Karel Král, *Working People in Czechoslovakia,* Prague, 1953, pp. 14–15 and ff.)

Such success does not generate a critical attitude. On the contrary, it led to toleration of arbitrary methods and the grave violations of law which were beginning to take place. But before we turn to the problems of the centralized model of socialism, let us add a few more indications of the accomplishment of the postwar years. This is essential to an understanding of why so few workers and intellectuals in 1968 agreed with those who argued that "twenty years have been lost."

Perhaps of most importance to the older workers was the far greater security of the new socialist system compared with that of the capitalism they had known. Unemployment was wiped out as had been promised. The frozen low rents, combined with this steady employment, made it possible for most workers to afford a decent flat for their families. Before the war a 1937 census had shown that 20 percent of the flats in Prague were vacant. Now with fewer people, flats suddenly could not be had and allocation became necessary on the basis of need. Free public medical care solved another great problem of insecurity. Vacations were extended, pensions raised, and after recovery from the serious 1947–48 drought, food supplies began to improve. The prices of essentials, such as bread and milk, were kept low.

Agriculture

We have mentioned agriculture only in passing because in the

---

[6] In the first postwar years these "závodní rady" had the political functions of watching former capitalist directors who still continued in the management of some enterprises. After 1948 these functions of trade unions fell into disuse.

first years there was comparatively little socialization of farming. The confiscated large estates were being broken up and the land distributed to private farmers. As late as 1950 only 11.1 percent of agricultural land was in cooperatives and another 10 percent in state farms. (Central Commission for People's Control and Statistics *Čísla pro každého* [*Data for Everyone*], SNTL, Prague, 1963, p. 91.) Yet in the mobilization of manpower the flow of workers out of agriculture into industry was of very great importance. According to the 1930 Census a total of 3,566,229 persons were "permanently employed" in agriculture. This figure includes children under 16. The census in September–October 1946 showed just about one million fewer or 2,588,629 employed in agriculture. (Glos, *op.cit.*, pp. 39–40.) By 1948 about 300,000 workers had been drawn from agriculture into industry and by 1966 the number was down to 1,257,000, so that farm employment in that year was not much more than a third the 1930 level. (*Czechoslovak Statistical Yearbook*, 1967, pp. 22–23.) As in any industry with sharply declining employment, the average age of those remaining tends to rise.[7]
Czechoslovak agriculture also had a serious problem in that half of all those remaining in agriculture were women, most of whom were not trained to handle machinery.

This age and sex structure of agricultural employment, combined with declining numbers, meant that *with the existing level of technology* a real shortage of agricultural manpower developed. With the shortage of labor in the rest of the economy this resulted in an acute pressure for a modernization of agriculture which would permit a rise in output and at the same time a further freeing of farm workers for other jobs. Before the war there was some very large-scale farming, but also much farming was on an ox-and-plow basis, and by modern standards was practically gardening in its use of labor power. At the end of the war Czechoslovak farms were fragmented into no less than 33 million plots. Sometimes one small farmer had as many as a dozen pieces of land scattered kilometers apart so that he spent a large part of his time

---

[7] By 1961 about 43.3 percent of those working in agriculture were 50 years or more of age. (ÚKLKS, *Statistická informace*, No. 152, 1962.) Even so, this was better than in the United States where the 1959 census showed that half of all farmers were 50 or more years of age and 17 percent were 65 years of age or older. (U. S. Department of Agriculture, *Fact Book of U. S. Agriculture*, 1965, p. 6.)

just going (at oxcart pace) from one field to another. Some of the fields (particularly in Slovakia) were only a few meters wide, and not a few were no larger than a tennis court. Such fragmentation precluded rational use of land, manpower, and machinery. Modern scientific agriculture required consolidated fields. This consolidation could be attained, as in the United States, by a process of ruthless competition that forces out the smaller farmers, or it could be attained by the formation of cooperatives and state farms. The Czechoslovaks chose cooperatives and state farms as being more humane and at the same time a method that permitted a rapid shift to socialist agriculture.

In theory, dating all the way back to Marx, the formation of cooperatives should have been voluntary, with farmers joining when it was shown to be in their interest to do so. Lip service was paid to this policy, but actually the rewards went to those who first could report "100 percent socialist farming" in their area. The result was pressures of all kinds, legal and illegal. Among the most effective was simply charging the recalcitrant farmer with large amounts of back taxes and classifying him as a "kulak" even though he had only a few hectares of land.[8] Many who refused to join went to prison, and these were often the most productive farmers. In fact, if they were foresighted and joined the cooperatives these "kulaks" often found themselves in leading positions. In general it can be said that capitalism forces out its least productive farmers. Collectivization—as practiced by the overeager city functionaries of the Party—forced out of farming in Czechoslovakia those who had the greatest knowledge of farming and had been most successful at it. From the beginning Czechoslovak cooperative farms struggled under an unnecessary load of resentment and bad feeling. They also suffered from loss of skilled people and correspondingly poorer leadership. It was assumed that any politically

---

[8] In Poland the methods of organizing and managing the farm cooperatives were so dictatorial and crude that the "cooperatives" disintegrated and had to be abandoned. Private farming was restored and even today dominates Polish agriculture. In the German Democratic Republic a very cautious agricultural policy was adopted and cooperative and state farms were slow in developing. Some German economists even list "the renunciation of the nationalization of the land" and "cooperation with loyal members of the bourgeoisie and big farmers in socialist transformation" as a major contribution of East Germans to the development of Marxist theory. (Adolf Bauer and Wolfgang Eichhorn, "The Basic Model of Socialism," *German Foreign Policy,* English edition, No. 1, 1969, p. 11.)

reliable mechanic could be an effective cooperative chairman—just as any group of Party people at the center could decide agricultural policy. This was one of many reasons for the great lag in the development of scientific farming.

The drive in Czechoslovakia to socialize agriculture took place in uneven spurts.[9] As we have seen, by 1950 about a fifth of the land was cultivated by the socialist sector and about half of this was in state farms. By 1953 a total of 6,679 cooperatives had been formed and the socialist sector of land had risen to 44.7 percent. But because not a few of the cooperatives had been organized under pressure and were badly managed, they soon fell apart. By 1954 the number of cooperatives was down to 6,502 and the proportion of land socially farmed was down to 41.9 percent.

Then a renewed pressure for increased agricultural productivity resulted in a further drive for cooperatives. A peak of 12,560 cooperatives was reached in 1959, with the socialized sector rising to 85.2 percent of the agricultural land. Many of these cooperatives were too small (even though they combined dozens of private farms) and did not have good management, so that gradually they were either absorbed into more successful cooperatives or their land was taken into state farms. In this process of enlarging the farms the number of cooperatives dropped from a 1959 peak to 6,395 in 1967, but the percentage of agricultural land in the socialized sector rose to 90.1 percent and included most of the land suitable for large-scale operations. In 1966 there were only 346 state farms but they farmed 20.8 percent of the land. The average size of the cooperatives in 1967 was 1,600 acres and of the state farms 8,770 acres. (*Statistical Yearbook,* 1968, pp. 35 and 304.) In general these farms were large enough to permit efficient use of machinery and good management. *This change to large-scale socialized units is a fundamental advance and lays the basis for modern scientific farming—but it does not guarantee that the actual farming will be highly productive and increasingly efficient.* In point of fact, some of the methods of centralized management were practical guarantees that the farming would atrophy and waste resources. We will return to this in the next chapter. Here we wish to underline that, despite the problems, socialist agriculture has

---

[9] Some of the early "cooperatives" were formed by larger farmers, suffering from a shortage of labor, in order to facilitate mechanization.

some creditable accomplishments. We can see this in the following table.

TABLE 2. Indices of Output per Worker and per Hectare, 1936–1969, Czechoslovakia

Year	1936	1948	1954	1958	1960	1962	1965	1969
Per worker	100	108	144	179	224	229	252	341
Per hectare	100	76	90	101	106	100	105	135

(ČSSR *Statistical Yearbook,* 1968, pp. 32–33, and 1971, p. 297.)

From this table we can see that in 1948, although output per hectare was about one-fourth less than in 1936, the number of workers had declined even more, so that productivity per worker was eight percent higher. By 1969, the average worker in agriculture was producing 3.4 times as much as in 1936—and doing so with a much shorter work day. But output per hectare showed no definite trend until after 1962. After that the trend became much more encouraging, but it still falls far below the potential of really scientific agriculture.

In Table 1 we saw that consumption of food (measured in constant prices) doubled in the years from 1948 to 1966, and this involved a considerable qualitative improvement as well as a leveling up of consumption among the different sections of the population. For example, in 1936 Czechoslovaks consumed an average of 34 kilos of meat per capita. By 1969 meat consumption was up to 69.7 kilos per person. Consumption of eggs per capita rose from 138 to 251 in the same period. (*Czechoslovak Statistical Abstract,* 1971, p. 462.)

Vegetable use showed a slight improvement, but milk product consumption declined. On the positive side, consumption of potatoes declined as did that of rye bread, while more wheat bread was consumed. Sugar consumption in the Czech lands rose from 25.8 to 39.5 kilograms, and in Slovakia from 15.2 to 35.6 kilograms per person. Total caloric intake per person averaged 2,545 in 1936 and 3,128 calories in 1968. (*Statistical Yearbook,* 1971, pp. 462–65.) Dieticians urge more milk, fruits, and green vegetables in the diet, but certainly the average food consumption is adequate in energy terms and its distribution is much more equalitarian than under capitalism.

Industrial Development

The strength of an economy can in part be judged by the number of tons of coal or steel or kilowatts of electricity it produces. Such tests, particularly the volume of electricity used per capita, tell us something about the level of development of an economy. But production of the means of production is not an end in itself and tells us little about the actual welfare of the people. It may be that investment in a new hospital or theater, or the subsidy for a string quartet or a new public swimming pool may add much more to the satisfaction of consumer needs than production of more coal or oil. Yet these are not classed as "productive" investment.

For many reasons Czechoslovak planners have used a large proportion of the national income for investments. (See Table 3.) In any one year, of course, this reduces the amount available for consumption, but if the project is effective, as soon as it is completed and the investment begins to be realized, the total amount available for consumption and further investment rises. We will discuss the question of the *efficiency* of the investment in the next chapter. In 1948 a total of 12.2 billion crowns, or about 11 percent of the national income, was invested. By 1967 a total of 70.4 billion, or roughly 30 percent of the national income, was invested. In real terms investments in 1967 were six times as high as they had been two decades before. By 1970 (in crowns of 1967 value) investments had soared to 88.5 billion crowns. (*Statistical Yearbook,* 1971, pp. 24–25.) Industry gets by far the largest part of the investment funds—33.6 billion crowns in 1970; followed by transport and communications, 10.9; agriculture, 9.4; housing, 15.8; schools, 3.5; science and research, 1.1; and construction, 3.2 billion crowns. Territorially, 60.3 billion was invested in the Czech area and 28.1 billion in Slovakia. (*Statistical Yearbook,* 1971, p. 208.)

Such large investments of course greatly expanded productive capacity (as well as cultural and other "nonproductive" facilities). In 1948 fixed assets in production had a value of 205 billion crowns. By 1965 they had reached more than 526 billion crowns. In industry fixed assets had increased from 115 to 320 billion crowns in that period (in 1955 prices). (*Statistical Yearbook,* 1966, p. 172.) The result was that in 1967 (on the eve of the 1968 upsurge of demand for political and economic change) the social product was 3.7 times greater and the national income[10] 3.3 times greater than that of 1948. (See Table 4.) In comparison, output of the means of production had increased by nearly 4.6 times, and this difference is only partly reflected in increased exports. It points a finger at one of the main problems, the increasing production for the sake of production, or a worsening of the input-output ratio.

TABLE 3. Trends of Investment 1948–1970, Czechoslovakia

Year	Investment, Billion Crowns[a]		Index, 1948 = 100	
	Investment, total	Investment in production	Investment, total	Investment in production
1948	12.2	8.2	100	100
1950	19.2	13.6	157	166
1953	28.9	19.1	237	233
1955	30.4	19.4	249	237
1958	42.2	30.5	346	372
1959	50.6	36.9	414	450
1960	56.6	41.3	465	504
1961	60.5	44.7	496	545
1962	58.8	43.7	482	533
1963	52.2	38.7	428	472
1964	58.2	43.4	477	529
1965	62.6	46.9	513	572
1966	68.6	52.0	563	634
1967	70.4	52.9	578	645
1968	76.2	56.8	625	693
1969	33.6	61.6	685	751
1970	84.5	61.8	725	754

[a] In constant prices of January 1, 1967.
Source: ČSSR Statistical Yearbook, 1971, pp. 24–25.

---

[10] Czechoslovak statistical classifications follow the Marxist terminology, and care must be taken in interpreting them by those used to other terminology. National income and social product as used here do not include the value of services not used directly in commodity production, for example, personal transport and education or medical care. But social product does not include (unlike national income) allowances for depreciation and includes the value of materials and products used in production. With the increasing specialization of production this means increased double counting. National income does not double count and therefore comes closer to representing the net value of commodity production. But the cost of services should be added before comparing with national income of countries using non-Marxist methods of calculation.

TABLE 4. Growth of National Income and Social Product, 1948–1970, Czechoslovakia

Year	National Income	Social Product	National Income	Social Product
	In billion crowns		(Index 1948 = 100)	
1948	70.2	130.6	100	100
1950	85.0	164.4	121	126
1951	93.1	179.1	133	137
1952	103.1	195.5	147	150
1953	109.7	206.9	156	158
1954	113.6	216.3	162	166
1955	125.3	238.4	178	183
1956	131.9	255.6	188	196
1957	141.5	274.7	202	210
1958	153.2	296.9	218	227
1959	162.9	319.1	232	244
1960	176.0	348.2	251	267
1961	188.2	372.9	268	285
1962	191.4	385.6	272	294
1963	185.0	382.5	266	294
1964	188.0	397.0	267	303
1965	194.4	416.3	277	319
1966	214.4	450.9	305	344
1967	233.7	563.9	326	370
1968	250.4	600.0	344	392
1969	265.7	628.9	365	410
1970	281.0	676.9	387	442

Source: ČSSR *Statistical Yearbook*, 1966, pp. 24–25 and 1971, pp. 24–25.

Gross industrial production in 1967 in current prices was 327,376 million crowns. But in 1966 prices it was only 263,341 million, indicating a wholesale price increase resulting from the 1967 "price reform" of about 24.2 percent. In real terms industrial production was about 5.5 times that of 1948. (*Statistical Yearbook*, 1968, pp. 28–29.) Such a rise of industrial production, together with an improvement in its quality, is of course the necessary basis for the rise in output and productivity of other parts of the economy, particularly agriculture, transport, and communication. These are impressive gains for the Republic as a whole. Territorially, in the development of industry in many places where there had been unemployment but relatively little industry, and for Slovakia as a whole, the relative gains were much greater. By 1967 industrial production in Slovakia was more than nine times the 1948 output and eighteen times the 1937 level. (*Ibid.,* p. 65.)

Most of this increase in total output has resulted from the increase in productivity of labor, not from growth in the number of workers, although that, too, was important until unemployment was wiped out. As we can see in Table 5, the population and the working force have increased, but compared to many other countries such as the United States or the Soviet Union, rather slowly. The total increase in employment from 1948 (when "full employment" was first attained) until 1967 was about 20.1 percent. In the same period overall social productivity of labor had increased by 3.1 times. A large part of this rise in productivity came from the shift of workers out of agriculture into industry. This made possible a rise in national income produced from 5,686 crowns per capita in 1958 to 16,336 in 1967. In this two-decade period, as we can see in Table 5, there was also a very large influx of workers into health services, education, and culture, indicating a considerable expansion of these services which contribute to the general welfare, but are not reflected in the national income data.

The larger expenditures for medical care, for culture, for pensions, as well as the absence of unemployment and of high differentials of incomes based on private ownership of property, made a qualitative difference in Czechoslovak society which must also be put down on the credit side for socialism. The emphasis on social equality, on the general need for educational and cultural opportunities for all members of society, and the effort to protect those without economic bargaining power from risks and misfortune, removed much of the strain and tension from the life of ordinary people. Unfortunately, as some tensions were removed others developed, particularly those related to the use of dictatorial methods of managing the economy and society.

It is not easy to put a price tag on such an item as the decline in infant mortality, or free medical care for all (a real item of communism since it is given on the basis of need), or security in old age, and in many of these respects Czechoslovakia is in the forefront of the nations of the world. But it was such comparisons with other, and mainly capitalist countries, which showed that large as these gains were, there was still cause for real dissatisfaction. Some of Czechoslovakia's neighbors were gaining even more in some fields, such as agriculture.

TABLE 5. Czechoslovak Population, Working Force and Employment by Major Occupation, 1948, 1958, and 1967 (in 000's)

	1948	%	1958	%	1967	%
Total population	12,000		13,474		14,305[a]	
Population of productive age	7,547		7,565		8,084	
Number employed, total	5,545	100	6,113	100	6,686	100
Agriculture	2,239	40.7	1,764	28.9	1,227	18.3
Industry	1,640	29.8	2,099	34.4	2,570	38.3
Construction	253	4.6	463	7.6	557	8.3
Trade	370	6.7	409	6.7	466	6.7
Health services and welfare	91	1.6	167	2.7	235	3.6
Education, culture, sport	138	2.5	262	4.3	398	5.9
National income produced, crowns per capita	5,686		11,367		16,336	

[a] The Czechoslovak population is now about stationary, being 14,334,000 in 1970.
Source: *ČSSR Statistical Yearbook*, 1968, pp. 22–25, 45, and 62.

Much other data could be added, but we think these will suffice to show that not only did socialism in Czechoslovakia have very important economic successes, but that a very firm basis of productive capacity has been built, and much additional construction is under way, which will make further advances technically possible. Expansion of the chemical industry gives promise of greater direct supplies of many consumer items—and also of much improved efficiency of other industries such as agriculture. At the same time, a serious mistake was made in following the concept that each country must develop a base in heavy industry. This mistake was the more serious because most of the investment in such heavy industry was of a type that was based on low-quality or inadequate natural resources and required large amounts of capital and manpower per unit of output. It was precisely these heavy industries that absorbed the largest investment and made the least efficient use of it, as we shall see shortly. To obtain a scientifically balanced picture of the economy, to understand why the centralized system of management must be changed, we should examine also the increasing complications and problems. The acute contradictions that developed require more than superficial explanation, since the pattern of many of them also appears in other socialist countries and cannot be related solely to personalities, the weather, or other transient influences.

Finally, looking ahead, the economic successes go far to offset the developing economic problems, so that it would be very one-sided to look for the causes of the revolutionary demands in 1968 solely in economic factors. It remained true, however, that the economic difficulties made the people much more aware of their political dissatisfactions until a point was reached when the political demands became an independent and reinforcing factor in the pressures for change.

CHAPTER 4

Breakdown in the Efficiency of Centralized Management

At the same time that the Czechoslovak economy was making real gains in number of workers employed, in national income, and in consumption of goods and services, a whole series of problems were developing. These were not just economic but also administrative and managerial, political and social. Let us first document some of the economic difficulties. We have seen that by 1967 national income in real terms was more than 3.2 times above the 1948 level. National income rose in a surprisingly even trend for the period up to about 1961 and then ran into such difficulties that it actually declined from 1962 to 1963 and was lower in 1964 than it had been in 1961. (See Table 4.) In real terms national income in 1962 had reached 191.4 billion crowns, dropped to 185.0 billion in 1963, was 188.0 billion in 1964, and rose to 194.4 billion in 1965. By 1970 it had soared to 281.0 billion crowns. (See Chart 1.)

Decline in the Efficiency of Investment

The stagnation in the development of national income from 1961 through 1964 was not because there had not been a large amount of investment in the economy and in industry itself. From 1953 to 1954 investments declined, but remained far above the 1948 level. In the four years 1961–64, direct investment in production reached the enormous total of 170.5 billion crowns (Table 3), but in 1964 national income was below that of 1961. This was a disastrous loss of efficiency and a failure of the plan to raise living standards by investment instead of consumption. In fact, national income turned down just when one would expect much new capacity for production to be coming into operation as the result of the high investments from 1959–1962. Yet national income did not respond. The widening gap between the inputs of investments and returns in the form of national income can be seen in Chart 1.

Another rough test of the effectiveness of investment is that of the number of crowns of investment funds needed to increase national income by one crown a year. Table 6 shows that in 1954 there was a sharp decline in efficiency of investment, partly because many large-scale and long-term projects had been undertaken on which no returns had yet been received.[1] In that year it took 3.6 crowns of investment to produce one additional crown of income. But this was a mild crisis compared to the expenditure in 1962 of 10.5 crowns to obtain each added crown of income. In 1963, 38,700,000,000 crowns were invested in productive capacity yet national income *declined* by 6.4 billion crowns! The high volume of *extensive* (labor-requiring) investments had so added to economic tensions and difficulties that the net product was actually reduced. In 1964 national income began to recover (Table 4) so that a ratio could again be calculated. It was 11.5 crowns of investment to one of income. By 1966 the efficiency of investment had recovered substantially and stood at 2.0. By 1970 it was back up above 4.0.

Despite the political upheaval, production in 1968 held up well and, as the charts show, national income increased substantially. But the *efficiency* of investment again declined after 1966, indicating that economic reform, cut off before it had a chance, is indeed essential. (See Table 6.)

A major cause of this inefficiency of investment was the persistent distortion of investments in favor of mining and heavy industry. These were precisely the industries with the lowest return of investment, as we can see in Table 7.

These data show that the number of crowns of investment required to add one crown of output annually in fuel (mainly coal) production increased from an average of 2.2 during 1956–60 to

---

[1] It is realized that some of the results of investment may occur in the same year as the investment. In other cases the return may not begin for up to a decade, as in the case of the Czechoslovak atomic reactor. But no attempt at lagging was made because of the lack of proper data and because the refinement would not substantially change the argument as demonstrated by these crude ratios. The recovery in 1966 and 1967 reflected the coming into production of some very large-scale investments, such as the beginning of operations of the East Slovak Steel Works. It may also have reflected the effects of the first steps in the introduction of the new system of management.

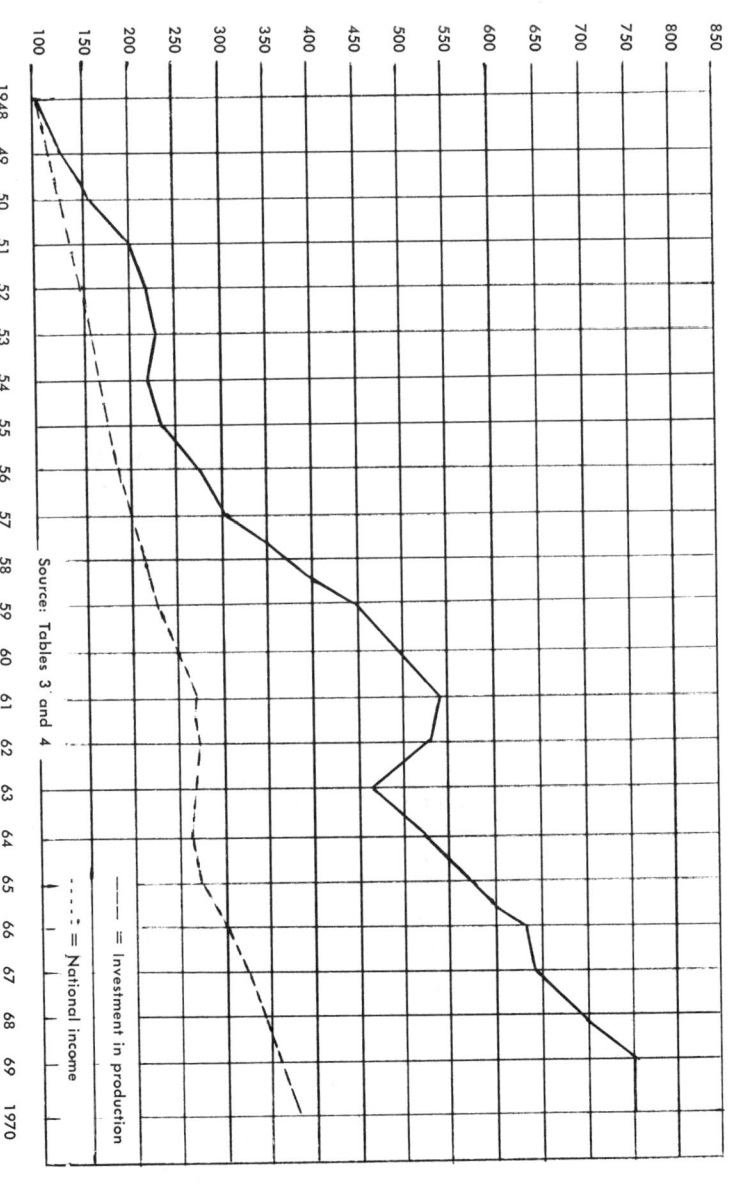

Chart 1. Indices of Growth of Czechoslovak National Income and Investment in Production (1948 = 100)

Source: Tables 3 and 4

——— = Investment in production
----- = National income

TABLE 6. Trends in Investment Costs per Increment of National Income

Year	Investment in production per crown of annual increment of National Income
1951	1.572
1952	1.483
1953	2.188
1954	3.570
1955	1.267
1956	2.631
1957	1.874
1958	2.000
1959	2.920
1960	2.423
1961	2.840
1962	10.531
1963	x
1964	11.460
1965	5.705
1966	2.005
1967	2.782
1968	3.401
1969	4.026
1970	4.039

x = not calculable.
Source: Calculated from data in Tables 3 and 4.

TABLE 7. Investment in Production per Increment of Gross Output, by Sectors of the Economy, Czechoslovakia

Ministry sphere	1956–1960	1961–1965	Percent of investment, 1965
Fuel	2.2	13.4	15.0
Electricity and heat	3.2	4.3	13.2
Steel and iron ore	1.4	4.1	14.7
Chemicals	1.7	2.2	11.0
Machinery	0.6	1.1	14.7
Construction	2.0	3.9	9.5
Consumer goods	0.7	1.8	9.8
Food	0.6	0.8	5.5

Sources: *Plánované hospodářství*, No. 10, 1965, p. 18; and *Statistical Yearbook*, 1966, pp. 153–55. The percentages of investment in 1965 do not add to 100 because the table does not include water projects which were not assignable to any specific ministry above.

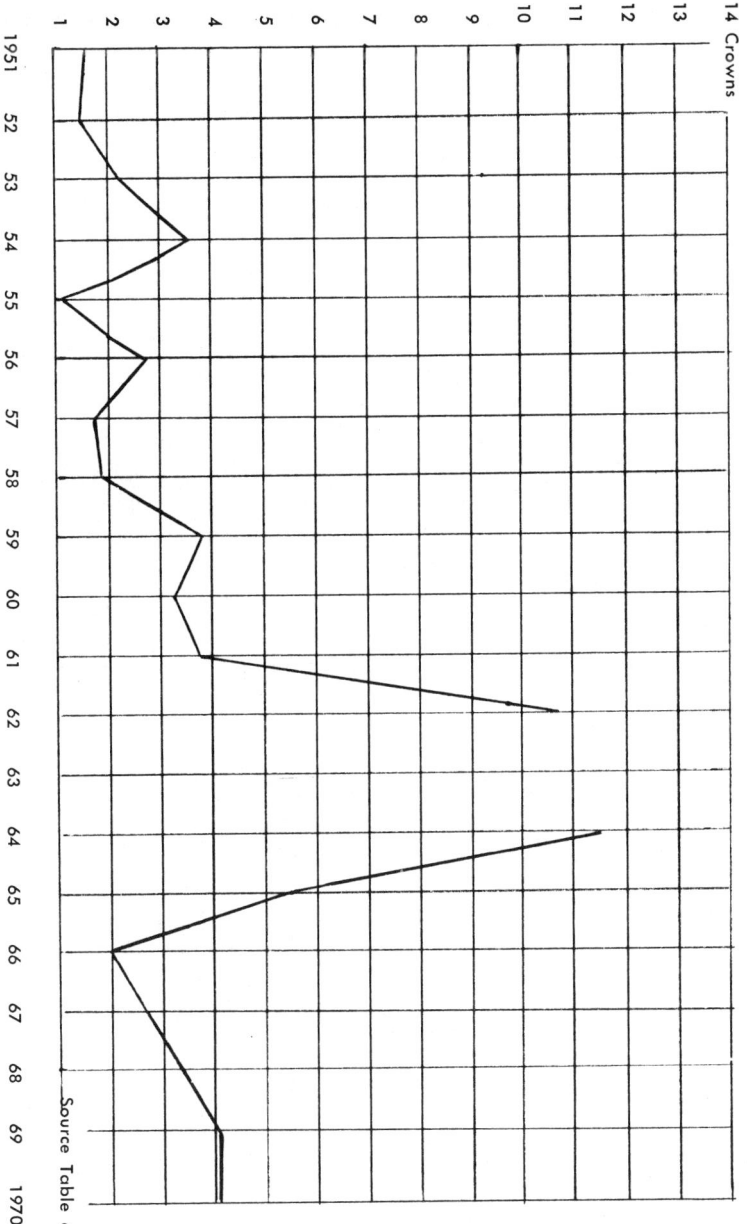

Czechoslovakia: Efficiency of Investment, 1951 to 1970

Chart 2. Crowns of Investment in Production Required to Produce One Crown Increment of National Income

Source Table 6

13.4 crowns in the years 1961–65. This was far more investment to achieve an increase in output than in any other sector—yet this was precisely the area of greatest investment! In contrast, consumer goods (includes textiles, clothing, leather, wood, paper, glass, porcelain, etc.) and food, where the return on investment was highest, received only 15.3 percent of the investments. For subjective reasons, the centralized planners were emphasizing investment in the industries that were least efficient *for Czechoslovakia*. The decline in efficiency was also much greater in those primary industries.[2]

From these data one must conclude that the central planners were certainly not optimizing the return on investment and came nearer to minimizing it. It may be argued that this is a false conclusion because the prices of the products did not reflect their true value, underrating the value of the products of heavy industry. But if this were so, it could only mean that the planners were operating in the dark, since without proper cost data there could be no scientific or rational plan of investment. Here we see the acute need not only for reliable accounting of costs, but also the constant need to compare cost data with those in the market, particularly the world market. Without this role of the market the planners have no way of knowing what real values are and hence can have no way of knowing which investments give optimal social returns. Once again, in light of these data, what could the so-called "Law of planned proportional development" mean?

It is of fundamental importance to note that this decline in efficiency of investment was not something unique to Czechoslovakia, but instead is characteristic of other centrally directed socialist economies. Let us take as an example of this three socialist economies with widely differing characteristics, Poland, the German

---

[2] It has been argued that one normally expects a lower rate of return in the basic industries and that therefore these data "prove nothing." This confuses rates of depreciation with rates of return. Further, it does not explain the sharp *decline* in rate of return from the earlier to the later period for such industries as fuel. The fact is that extensive (labor-using) investments continued to be made in heavy industry as a matter of subjective policy, even though the specific resources of Czechoslovakia did not justify them. It was not just the industry selected, but the type of investment within that industry. A whole new steel-making complex was built up near Košice in Slovakia when what was needed was more rolling and fabricating capacity. Labor-using investments were emphasized when labor-saving investments were needed.

Democratic Republic (G.D.R.), and the Soviet Union. In the following table we see the increase in annual national income per unit of investment in the sphere of production. Note that these data reveal a sharp and long-term decline in efficiency of investment in each of the three countries.

TABLE 8. Decline in the Effectiveness of Investment: Poland, the German Democratic Republic, and the Soviet Union, 1951–1965. Increment of national income per unit of investment in production.

Years	Poland	German Democratic Republic	Soviet Union
1951–55	0.44	0.85	0.75
1956–60	0.35	0.42	0.56
1961–65	0.29	0.18	0.38

Source: Z. Chalupský and others, "Z výsledků analýz faktorů ekonomického rozvoje členských zemí RVHP" (Results of the Analysis of Factors of Economic Growth Among Members of the COMECON), Československá a Slovenská společnost ekonomická při ČSAV, *Bulletin* No. 2, July 1968, pp. 113–15.

These are five-year periods so they rule out most temporary or accidental factors in the trends. If we push the period back to include 1948–50 we find the decline in efficiency of investment in Poland even greater, for then one zloty of investment produced an increase of 1.22 zlotys of annual income. We do not have earlier data for the G.D.R. and Soviet Union, but the trend is clear. The greater reserves of labor power in Poland are indicated by the fact that in 1960 some 47 percent of workers were engaged in agriculture, in the Soviet Union the percentage was 35, while in the G.D.R. in that year it was 17.6. (Chalupský, *loc. cit.*, p. 112.) In Czechoslovakia in 1970 only 13.7 percent of the workers were in agriculture. In the Soviet Union the number had dropped abruptly to 20 percent in 1970. (*Kommunist,* Moscow, No. 7, 1971.)

From these data we see that the least developed country, Poland, had the smallest decline in efficiency of investment, while the most developed industrially, the German Democratic Republic, suffered the greatest decline—from a ratio of 0.85 to only 0.18. One reason for this is that in general these were investments requiring large amounts of manpower, and of this Poland and the Soviet Union had comparatively large reserves in agriculture, while those in the German Democratic Republic, like those in Czechoslovakia, are comparatively small. Now that the Soviet Union has about exhausted this source of manpower, new, labor-saving forms of management are required.

As late as 1958 in Czechoslovakia the ratio of income to investment was 50 hellers of income for each crown invested (this is the reciprocal of the ratio shown in Table 6). But in 1964, the last full year before some measures of economic reform, one crown of investment produced less than a fifth as much income (0.096 of a crown).

These trends stand by themselves, but since we are concerned not only with internal efficiency but also with competition with the capitalist countries, a few comments on comparative trends are also significant. Of course trends vary a great deal in the different countries and we have no intention of examining all of the reasons for this. If we compare Czechoslovakia with the two capitalist countries that border on it we see the following:

TABLE 9. Growth of National Income per Unit of Net Investment

Years	Czechoslovakia	Austria	West Germany
1951–55	0.56	0.53	0.59
1956–60	0.39	0.35	0.34
1961–65	0.10	0.24	0.22

Source: Calculated by Economic Institute, Czechoslovak Academy of Sciences from official *Yearbook* data, *Srovnávací studie a životní úroveň v ČSSR, NSR a Rakousku* (Comparison of Living Standards in Czechoslovakia, the German Federal Republic, and Austria), Prague, 1967, p. 17.

Here we see that in the years 1951–55 the effectiveness of investment in Czechoslovakia was about on a par with that in the two neighboring capitalist countries. The effectiveness declined in all three countries, but more in Czechoslovakia, so that in the period 1961–1965 investments were only half as efficient as in Austria and West Germany. Note that "national income" in Czechoslovakia does not include the value of services, while in Austria and West Germany it does. This tends to understate the comparative gains in Czechoslovakia.

We should not conclude from this that a decline in efficiency of investment is inherent either in socialism or in advancing technology—in fact new technology permits an increase in efficiency of use even of land, used by the classical English economists to illustrate the law of diminishing returns. In the United States the efficiency of all inputs into agriculture, with 1935=100, rose from about 84 in 1910 to around 150 in 1960. (Hans Lansberg, *Natural Resources for U. S. Growth,* Johns Hopkins, 1964, p. 151.) John W. Kendrick calculated that the productivity of all factors of production in the United States in 1957 was 79 percent higher than in 1929. But no increase in the efficiency of *capital* inputs had occurred after 1944. (U. S. Department of Commerce, Bureau of the Census, *Long Term Economic Growth, 1860–1965,* USGPO 1966, p. 189. This is a basic publication on U. S. economic growth, with extensive bibliography, discussion of methods, and international comparisons.) At this writing no comparable data are available for the efficiency of capital inputs after 1957.

If we look at the diversity of trends in the effectiveness of investment in the different capitalist countries we must conclude that the quality and form of management have a great deal to do with the efficiency of use of new technology. Some of the capitalist countries are making huge investments and yet are able to avoid a sharp decline in the return of investment. Planners in socialist countries can get little comfort from comparative data on investments and returns in the capitalist countries. They must stick to their knitting and tackle the problem of efficiency of investment in their own countries.

This is perhaps most obvious in the case of agriculture. Ivan Volvochenko, First Deputy Minister of Agriculture in the Soviet Union, in 1968 first pointed to increased agricultural production and then added:

> While total production *expenditures* on the collective farms rose by 55 percent between 1961 and 1966, total *output* rose by only 11 percent.
> (*Ekonomika Selskovo Khozyaistva,* No. 3, 1968.)

In this same article he noted that in such a standard operation as plowing the costs per hectare rose 32.6 percent from 1962 to 1966, with "extremely low utilization of the tractor fleet." *(Ekonomika Selskovo Khozyaistva,* No. 3, 1968.)

Similarly, Leonid Brezhnev, in reporting to the Communist Party Central Committee on Soviet agriculture in March 1965, remarked that in 1955–59 the average annual rate of growth of agriculture had been 7.6 percent, but that during the last five years it had been only 1.9 percent. (*Pravda,* March 27, 1965.)

A year later Brezhnev told the 23rd Congress of the Communist Party:

> The rate of growth of production and of labor productivity has slowed down somewhat in recent years. The efficiency of production assets and the effectiveness of capital investments have dropped. There were delays in starting up new enterprises in some branches, and many of the new factories have not attained their rated capacity. As a result, the rate of growth of the national income fell short of the seven-year plan target.
> The reasons for these negative facts stem from the deficiencies of economic management, the underrating of scientific methods of management and of economically effective production, incomplete use of material and moral stimuli, the miscalculations in planning and a subjectivist approach to the solution of some economic problems.
> (*Pravda,* April 9, 1966.)

Here, in the declining effectiveness of investment, we have *one* fundamental reason why all of the developed socialist countries must seek, and are seeking, new methods of management which make more effective use of invested resources.

Waste of Capacity

One reason that quality was uneven and that productivity lagged behind the planned potential was that under the centralized plan with fixed output targets, the actual production took place in surges of activity that mounted as the terminal date of the plan neared, and then dropped abruptly just after the deadline was passed, only to resume its upward swing again. Often these fluctuations were quite violent, in some cases with a third more being produced in the last period of the plan than in the first. This "storming" was a phenomenon in all of the centrally planned economies, and thousands of articles were written about it, explaining and deploring it.

In 1951 Jaromír Dolanský, Minister-Chairman of the Czechoslovak State Planning Office, said:

Breakdown in the Efficiency of Centralized Management 49

We must, willy nilly, cope with the problem of "storming." We must begin a fight against the practice of delaying the fulfillment of the plan at the beginning of the period (whether it be a year, a month, or a week) and then hastily catching up at the end of the period. One of the most effective means of overfulfillment of the plan would be to remove these elements of storming and irregularity. You all know that this storming is one of the most wasteful and costly ways of meeting the plan. Overcoming the storming is also one important means of lowering the costs of production and of increasing the productivity of labor. Storming leads to unused equipment and manpower, to unused capacity, to waste of materials, to an increasing number of rejects and to an uneconomical increase of wages by overtime pay. . . . Storming also undermines socialist emulation and results in a feverish situation in which there is danger of non-fulfillment of the plan.
(*Plánované hospodářství,* No. 3–4, March–April 1951, pp. 134–35.)

This was a rather thorough indictment of management methods, and some specific steps were taken to overcome the fluctuations, among them the general banning of payment for overtime. But storming persisted, as can be seen in Chart 3. Aside from February which has fewer work days, and July and August in which whole factories shut down for vacations, a definite pattern exists of increasing industrial output in the last months of each plan quarter and at the end of the year as the yearly plan comes to a close. In 1963 industrial output in the last quarter of the year was 17.5 percent higher than in the first—and within those quarters there were further variations. In 1964 industrial output in the last quarter was 13.6 percent above that of the first quarter.

This evidence shows that for industry as a whole *at least* 10 percent of capacity was unutilized during parts of the year. If in addition we count the costs in lowered work morale, in waste of materials and increased rejects, this represents a serious indictment of management methods being used. We conclude that this problem was not solved, despite all the attention given to it, because the Party refused to permit the consideration of fundamental solutions. As long as the enterprises were operating on the "cost plus" basis

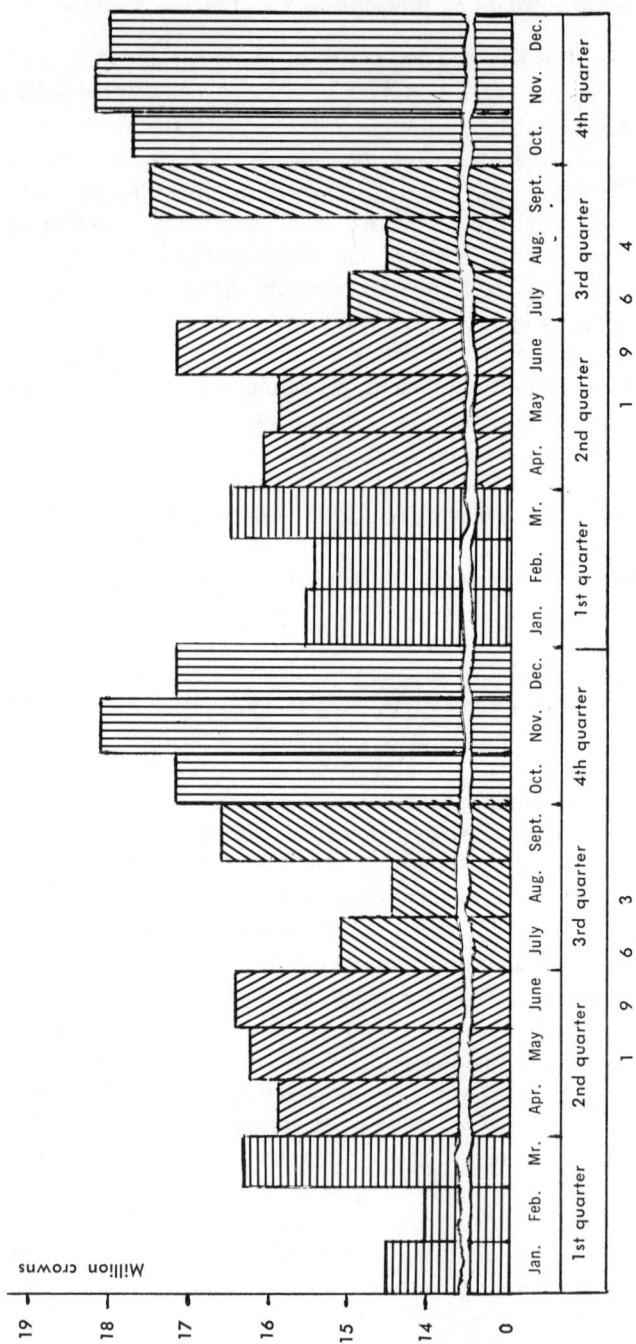

Chart 3. Czechoslovakia: Variations in Industrial Output According to Terminal Dates of Plan, 1963 and 1964

Source: Czechoslovak Planning Office data.

of plan fulfillment they had too weak incentives to be concerned with using capacity efficiently, and in fact had counterincentives to such efficiency. And, as we have seen and will come back to again below, no effective rewards for improving quality exist under the old-style plan.

Prohibition of payment of overtime removed one of the incentives for storming. However, one effect of the prohibition of overtime wages was that it resulted in an inflexibility of use of labor power that sometimes was costly. After the Slapy Dam on the Vltava River had been completed, and the turbines had been installed, but before the current had begun to flow to Prague, I noted that the workday seemed to be ending at 2:30 in the afternoon. With only a few more days' work the project would have been finished, yet there was no hurry, since no overtime was being paid. The Party leader on the project was quite content, pointing out that the dam would soon save about 3,200 tons of coal a day. But he did not agree that it would be good policy to pay some overtime and speed the day when that saving would begin. So, for days unused water poured over the spillway while the losses mounted to hundreds of thousands of crowns. Similarly, on the Vah River a new Kaplan turbine was being disassembled after a few days of operation for a "routine factory inspection." No one at all appeared to be working on the inspection and the local director estimated that the inspection would take at least three weeks. Here a faulty concept of costs was operating. Moreover, and this was the decisive thing, no one had an economic interest in seeing that the social loss of idle equipment was minimized. The entire social investment had been made, but no one was responsible and suitably rewarded for seeing that the investment was realized as quickly as possible.

A similar situation prevailed throughout the construction industry: premiums were paid for completion of *parts* of projects, and sometimes as many as 16 contractors worked on one project. Since considerable progress had been made in the technique of excavation, yet centrally fixed contract prices remained unchanged, this was the most profitable part of a building. So we found a proliferation of excavations and of partly completed construction. The finishing work was more poorly paid, so many houses remained uninhabitable for months because the electrical work or plumbing had not been finished—although most of the contractors had long since been paid off.[3]

Waste of Materials

With the rapid advance of science, new materials become available and new methods of using them become possible. Some of these make possible enormous savings in material costs. There are thousands of opportunities for such savings arising in new forms almost daily. Among these are the substitution of more effective or easier-to-process materials, such as plastics for metals; substitution of metal forming for metal cutting; miniaturization; substitution of transistors, diodes, etc. for electronic tubes; and substitution of printed circuits for wiring. One test of the alertness of management to the use of new technology is the trend of materials costs per unit of output. Particularly in the newer electronics commodities the weight of the product in relation to its value has declined sharply. Since many of the new elements used are rare or costly to process, every effort is made to increase the efficiency of their use and to cut the weight and bulk of the machines and equipment in relation to their capacity. Success can no longer be measured in terms of tons of materials produced, but in low consumption of such materials in relation to capacity of the machinery produced or of the consumer goods marketed.

This is why we must look closely at the following table which shows the declining global efficiency in use of materials in relation to the resulting social product in Czechoslovakia (Table 10). In 1948 the value of materials used in production including depreciation but not labor power was 60.4 thousands million crowns, or 46.3 percent of the social product. The cost of materials in relation to the social product rose gradually, but was still under 50 percent as late as 1960. Then it rose rapidly, reaching the huge total of 330.2 thousand million crowns in 1967. This was 58.6 percent

---

[3] The trend just before August 1968 was toward one responsible contractor, and perhaps, after the Intercontinental Hotel Prague experience, even toward competitive bidding for large construction contracts. There a United States contractor was the builder, and insisted on competitive bidding. To the surprise of the Czechs a big difference in bids resulted. The workers were promised good bonuses for good work—and got none the first pay day. After looking at films of themselves at work, all but 27 workers agreed that they had not deserved the bonuses. The 27 were fired and replaced by others and the work proceeded at a much brisker pace.

TABLE 10. Decline of Efficiency: Materials used in Production in Relation to Gross Social Product

Year	Materials used in production[a] (in thousand million crowns)	Share of gross social product[b]
1948	60.4	46.3
1950	79.3	48.3
1951	86.0	48.0
1952	92.4	47.3
1953	97.2	47.0
1954	102.7	47.5
1955	113.1	47.5
1956	123.7	48.4
1957	133.2	48.5
1958	143.7	48.4
1959	156.2	49.0
1960	172.2	49.4
1961	189.6	52.3
1962	198.1	53.0
1963	201.5	54.0
1964	212.2	55.1
1965	227.1	56.0
1966	240.8	55.0
1967	330.2	58.6
1968	349.0	58.5
1969	363.2	57.7
1970	395.9	58.5

[a] Productive consumption including depreciation.
[b] Ratio between productive consumption and the gross social product.
Source: ČSSR *Statistical Yearbook,* 1968, pp. 24–25, and 1971, pp. 24–25.

of the social product—or 12.3 points above 1948. This meant that the *added* cost of materials in 1967 was more than 40,000,000,000 crowns—over 2,600 crowns for every person in Czechoslovakia. These are data for industry as a whole and reflect both the declining efficiency in use of materials in many enterprises and also the structural shift of the economy to industries that required large inputs of materials. After 1967 the ratio remained almost unchanged, but the materials used, and wasted, increased.

This was not the only bad result of the rising trend of material costs. The higher costs of materials usually did not add to the usefulness or saleability of the product, but instead often detracted from it. A machine tool that weighs 25 percent more than its competitor with the same capacity is certain to sell for less—if it sells at all.

Czechoslovak experience points to the fact that excessive weight is a good index of general bad design or, more precisely, of failure to improve design, and this may mean a more than proportionate decline in selling price. In 1966 Czechoslovak machinery exports were commanding only about two-thirds of the price per kilo of capitalist competitors. The loss becomes obvious in this external competition, but the failure to innovate is a social cost over the entire internal consumption. This was brought out in a discussion by Soviet Academician Alexander Tselikov:

> An analysis shows that 18 to 25 percent more metal is being used per unit of engineering in our country [the Soviet Union] than in some other countries. Engineering is using about 50 million tons of metal a year. Consequently, in excessive waste, and in excessive weight of machines we are losing 9 to 12 million tons of metal a year.
>
> If we add the excessive waste of metal used in other industries and in construction, this figure will grow considerably. In short, the unjustified use of metal in our country is equal in volume to the production of metal in such a big country as Italy. Why does this take place? First of all because the workers in engineering do not pay sufficient attention to reducing the weight of machines, and especially in reducing the waste of metal in the preparatory operations.
>
> (*Pravda,* Moscow, September 13, 1968, p. 2.)

We cannot be satisfied with this answer. The real question is *why* the engineers, in a centrally managed socialist economy, do not respond to such repeated exhortations and design machines that not only equal those of their capitalist competitors but excel them. Marxists should not berate individuals for a common pattern of behavior, but look to the underlying reasons for that behavior.

In a country such as Czechoslovakia that sells a large part of the machines that it produces on the world market, the extra cost and weight of materials in the product are a double handicap: the product is less desirable, and it costs more. In the world market there is no protection of the seller (in this case the Czechoslovak *people,* not the producing enterprise) from the effects of higher costs and lower quality. The product sells for less, the net income for the seller is much less.

The waste of materials was a double disaster for Czechoslovakia because she imported a large part of those materials, and this involved an increasing amount of production in order to be able to import more materials—and when the quality of the final product fell behind the changing and improving quality of competing products, it sometimes meant that the income realized from the exported commodity was not as great as the cost of the materials imported! The social effect of this was a waste of all of the productive effort involved in the export, or, in Alice-in-Wonderland terms, of having to run faster and faster just to stay in the same place.

This *relative* increase in materials costs and in other costs in relation to quality and types of products can best be shown in regard to the world market. In 1948 Czechoslovak costs of production and export prices were about on the level with those of the nonsocialist world market, admittedly a far from perfect touchstone. Trading was carried on profitably with no state subsidies. By 1955 Czechoslovak domestic prices (and, presumably, costs) were about 58 percent above capitalist world prices, and by 1963 they were approximately double world prices.[4] These are only rough estimates, but, quality considered, are close to the trend. Many items of export could be sold only on the basis of price concessions, and in turn the difference between the internal costs and the export price had to be made up by adjustments of the state budget.

In fact these manipulations of export prices and payments to the producing firms became so complex that no one knew for sure just what costs were, which firm was being subsidized, and which was producing at a social gain. One economist, Jan Pleva, who studied these cost-export problems intensively, remarked that the

---

[4] Readers of English will find a summary discussion of these problems in Josef Goldmann and Karel Kouba, *Economic Growth in Czechoslovakia*, Academia, Prague, 1969, pp. 85 and ff.; for those who can read Czech, the original discussion and calculations are of interest and may be found in Jan Pleva, "Některé problémy zahraničního obchodu," Economic Institute, CSAV, Vyzkumná pub. No. 15, 1966, pp. 119 and ff.; also Jan Klacek and Jan Pleva, "Efektivnost zahraničně obchodních operací na trhu," *Politicka ekonomie*, No. 7/8, 1967.

subjective and arbitrary setting of internal prices without regard to socially necessary costs or world prices, in the end produced such a baffling distortion of prices, such departures from value, that it was impossible to know what costs actually were. "It was like looking into the reflections in a set of distorted mirrors and trying to guess what the original image was like."

The other side of the rising share of the social product required for materials (including depreciation) is the declining share available for consumption. Much of what is nominally "produced" and already counted as a part of "national income" may in fact not be available either for consumption or productive investment. This is the case of the rise in the amount of unfinished capital construction and the excessive accumulation of inventories. Jaroslav Budín has estimated that in 1966–67 about 50 percent of the rise in national income actually went into the accumulation of stocks. (Budín, "The Position of Czechoslovakia in the World Economy," Plánované hospodářství, No. 9, 1968.) Goldmann and Kouba calculate that the expenditures for increase in inventories and for increments of unfinished capital projects absorbed no less than a third of the rising volume of capital formation of the economy. (*Op. cit.*, pp. 68 and 72–73.) They concluded that this was one major factor in the decline in the growth rate of the economy.

They also noted that the decline in long-term growth rate in Czechoslovakia was similar to that in several other of the socialist economies. In general terms their rate of growth was about one-half as high in 1968 as it had been in 1953. In the Soviet Union, for example, the annual increment of industrial development had been 23 percent in 1953 and 16 percent in 1951, but had dropped to 9 percent in 1965 and 8 percent in 1968. (*Ibid.*, pp. 62–63 and Central Statistical Board of the U.S.S.R., *Report,* January 22, 1969.) The increase of industrial output for 1971 was 7.8 percent and for national income 6.0 percent. (*Pravda,* January 23, 1972.) Note that these are still high rates of growth by historical standards, but we must be concerned also with the trends, and the reasons for the trends.

Productivity of Labor

If we turn from the efficiency of use of materials and capital investments to the trends in productivity of labor we find once more both success and mounting problems. In Table 11 we can trace the year-by-year development of labor productivity (as measured by growth of the national income per worker) for the economy as a whole and for industry, construction, and agriculture. As we have noted, the overall increase in productivity in the two decades from 1948 to 1967 was more than threefold. But from 1953 to 1954 there was almost no change in productivity, with the small rise in industry offsetting the decline in agriculture. Then for seven years there was no improvement in output per worker in agriculture—in fact the index (1948 = 100) in 1959 was only 148 and it had been as high as 154 in 1953. Then, with sharply rising inputs of fertilizers and machinery, the trend was once more rising, although there were bad years in 1962 and 1965.

The difficulties with productivity per worker in construction became obvious only after 1960 when the index of productivity was well above double (219) that of 1948. By 1963 productivity was down to only 182 and, although it improved in 1964 it was only two points above the level reached in 1959! In industry productivity in 1961 was just double (201) that of 1948—but by 1964 it was still only 201. Here is an indicator of real trouble, because if productivity does not rise (despite enormous investments) real wages cannot rise and national income per capita will stagnate. (See Table 4.)

Academician Ota Šik commented:

The growth of productivity of human labor gradually slowed down during the past years, mainly because on a nationwide average the technical basis of production was not sufficiently improved and the average age of machinery grew. The replacement of machinery in the existing old factories, where experienced workers predominated, was insufficient and the decisive portion of depreciation funds was used, together with net investment funds, for expanding and building new factories and shops. But, even in the new enterprises, the technical standard of the machinery and equipment was not such as to ensure the necessary thorough changes in production technology and, together with the undermanning and insufficient training of the newly hired manpower, the result was that for years many new enterprises did not even attain the productivity of the old enterprises.

(Šik, *New Trends in Czechoslovak Economics,* No. 2, March 1967, pp. 17–18.)

An educated people like the Czechs and Slovaks know that socialism can and must do better than the performance of the economy after 1961. The discontent was not just with the failure of the standard of living to rise, despite all the investments poured into industry and agriculture, but was increasingly linked also to social and political difficulties. In fact, political unrest began even while the economy was still operating in a generally satisfactory manner. It was the ordinary resentment of intelligent people against dictatorial methods. This unrest became more open after the death of Stalin and particularly after the revelations, in 1956, at the 20th Congress of the Communist Party of the Soviet Union. One specific demand at that time of a large number of members of the Czechoslovak Communist Party was that a special congress be called to democratize the rules and methods of their own Party. First Secretary Antonín Novotný[5] succeeded in frustrating this attempt, but the fundamental demand for democracy remained latent with the people. This unrest over the economic-political results of socialism had a dangerous aspect in that many people were inclined to blame the failures on socialism as such and not on the particular centralized and dictatorial model of it that was in force in Czechoslovakia.

One crisis in this alienation from socialism came when the Third Five-Year Plan, which was to run from 1961 through 1965, had to be abandoned in 1962. That Plan had been drawn up by teams of experts working thousands of hours and using the latest techniques to balance out the uses of resources in an optimal way, to determine the share of incomes going to investments, the flows of materials and uses of productive capacities, the shares for consumption and services. It was the most elaborate plan yet drawn up.

---

[5] Antonín Novotný, born near Prague in 1904, was a machinist by trade. Early in life he became active in the trade unions and Communist Party. For this he was imprisoned by the Nazis in Mauthausen. After the War he returned to Prague where he became first district secretary and then First Secretary of the Central Committee. Upon the death of President Antonín Zápotocký in 1957, Novotný became President of the Republic, while retaining the key post of First Secretary. He was also First Secretary of the National Front, a formidable amount of power and an enormous load of duties for one man.

TABLE 11. Social Productivity of Labor, Czechoslovakia, 1948 to 1970

Year	Total[a]	In industry	In construction	In agriculture
1948	100	100	100	100
1950	122	109	86	146
1951	135	119	90	139
1952	148	128	124	142
1953	155	132	136	154
1954	156	133	136	132
1955	170	144	158	144
1956	180	152	173	143
1957	192	159	179	150
1958	208	172	184	158
1959	225	182	202	148
1960	246	189	219	170
1961	262	201	220	176
1962	264	206	210	149
1963	260	201	182	176
1964	263	201	204	171
1965	271	209	225	148
1966	291	217	259	178
1967	305	224	271	199
1968	321	233	272	221
1969	338	247	266	235
1970	349	265	272	213

[a] The greater rise in overall productivity, compared with the major industries shown, results from the shift from less productive to more productive industries. For example, shifts of workers out of agriculture, where annual production per worker in 1966 was only 15,100 crowns, into industry where it was 52,500 crowns, would result in an increase in total productivity greater than that shown for either industry. (Computed from *Statistical Yearbook* by Vladimír Nachtigal, Economic Institute, Academy of Sciences, Prague.)

Source: ČSSR *Statistical Yearbook,* 1971, pp. 24–25.

Yet, within a comparatively short time after it had been drawn up it became evident that it could never be carried to completion. In a way it was, to put it bluntly, a vast exercise in bureaucratic self-deception. It failed because some of its basic premises were wrong. Its framers had postulated both a large increase in total number of workers and a very high rate of increase in productivity of labor. The planning experts knew that automation and all the other new technologies made *possible* such advances. What they did not realize was that the centralized administrative model would encourage extensive investments and inhibit labor-saving and materials-saving innovation at a time when the economy no longer had the resources for extensive growth. What was needed was a demonstration of the often repeated assertion that socialism could use automation far more effectively than capitalism. What was needed was a plunge into the technology of the future. What the centralized model reproduced was more of the past.

CHAPTER 5

Reasons for the Failure of Centralized Management

We have seen that the Third Five-Year Plan broke down in 1962 shortly after the elaborate work of preparing it had been completed. This was not the failure of individual planners or ministers or engineers, but the result of the economic model with which they were working. When we examine the reasons for this failure in planned management we see a tangled skein of many economic and political threads, and if we try to trace them out we find them leading repeatedly back and through each other in a most baffling manner with seemingly no beginning or end. Yet, if we persist we will find main lines of influence and definite patterns of cause and effect. The most important of these was the failure of the system as such to *require* technological innovation, and the second and, in a real sense, the other side of this was the failure to use all resources, including labor power, to optimum advantage.

The Third Five-Year Plan postulated extensive investments in new plants, more construction and housing, more services, and more students attending higher institutions of education. All of these required manpower, materials, and imports. In order to make the plan balance, the planners postulated increases both in total manpower and in its productivity—big increases of both. The plan assumed that employment in the socialized sector of the economy (not counting the farm cooperatives) would increase by about 440,000 in the five-year period and that productivity of labor in industry would increase by 43 percent, in construction by 54 percent, and in agriculture by 53 percent. (*Plánované hospodářství*, No. 12, 1960, pp. 889–90.)

Let us start with the quantity of labor. In capitalist countries one characteristic marking the end of the boom phase of the economic cycle is the decline in labor productivity as the demand for it rises and draws into the working force less qualified and less diligent workers. This is one major cause of the rise in unit costs of output and of the decline in the rate of profit, or of "efficiency of investment." Generally, a high rate of employment is accompanied over a period of years by an easing of the pressure on those employed to turn out a high amount of work and an increasing difficulty in enforcing norms for both quantity and quality of output. Yet what is regarded as a very high rate of employment for capitalism, even as "full employment," is far below the proportion of the population of employable age that has been working in Czechoslovakia since 1948. In the United States in the very good year of 1960 the proportion of those employed to the total population 14 years of age or over was 55 percent. (U. S. *Statistical Abstract,* 1967, p. 221.) In Czechoslovakia the roughly corresponding percentage in 1961 was 79.9 percent—and by 1965 it had risen to a fantastic 82 percent. (ČSSR, *Statistical Yearbook,* 1967, pp. 22–23 and 111.) There can be no doubt that the problem of unemployment had been solved!

But in generating the excessive demand for labor, in the competition for workers with which to meet the goals of the plan, not only were less qualified workers used, but a strain was put on the whole culture, with many women with young children attempting to do the double duty of raising a family and holding a job. Even if the child is in a nursery school the results are often bad both for the factory and for the family. If the child becomes ill it has to stay home and the mother with it. Attendance at work is irregular and the scheduling of the flow of work more difficult. The strain on the woman is high, and many psychologists are beginning to doubt if such a regime of nursery-school–working-mother is worth the gain in commodity output.

On the part of the men, such a high level of employment also had adverse effects, as can be seen in the case of construction where they constitute the largest part of the workers. There the fact that if a worker was fired he could go around the corner and get another job, reduced work morale; absences increased; and the volume of idle time mounted. We have seen (Table 11) that the index of productivity in construction dropped from 220 in 1961 (1948=100) to only 182 in 1963. Such a *decline* is closely related to the recruitment of an additional 268,000 construction workers from 1948 to 1961, or more than double the original number. (It was in serious trouble again from 1967 through 1970 when productivity did not rise at all.)

Surprisingly, the Third Five-Year Plan achieved comparatively greater success in recruiting additional workers than it did in improving their productivity. The Plan postulated an increase of 440,000 workers—and by the end of 1965 more than 650,000 workers had actually been added to the work force. Of these *some 436,000 were women. (Plánované hospodářství,* No. 12, 1960, p. 890, and ČSSR, *Statistical Yearbook,* 1967, p. 111.)

This extensive development of the labor supply brought with it, as we have just argued, serious problems of work morale, general qualifications of the recruits, and the resulting effect on productivity of labor.

Important as it was, the decline in qualifications and morale was not the main cause of unsatisfactory productivity. We must remember that while many less qualified persons were being drawn into the labor force, many highly educated specialists were also being added. The general level of education of Czechoslovak workers had seldom, if ever, been equaled in any country. The question is: Why were not these workers used to greater advantage? Why did productivity decline just at a time when society could have used its increase to full advantage? The key to higher productivity does lie partly in work norms and in intensity of manual and intellectual effort, but the main factor around the world in the long-term trend of rising productivity is new technology. And we must look for the explanation of the failure of productivity to rise (Table 11) as expected by the Third Plan to the failure of the overcentralized economic model to promote innovation of technology, to *require* the development of automation and other labor-saving equipment and methods.

Instead, the operating pressures in the plan persistently forced extensive development, and this stretched almost intolerably the resources of labor power. When the planned rises of productivity were not realized because of the lag in technological innovation, some firms began to fail to meet their quantity targets in the plan. Once this took place in a tightly interlocked plan that had few *apparent* and no planned reserves of labor power or other capacity, the repercussions spread widely throughout the economy. A failure of one plant to produce the amount or quality of raw material planned resulted in the failure of its customer plant to fulfil its plan. Once the breakdown of the plan began, it multiplied the difficulties of plan administration in a geometrical ratio: one failure produced many complications, complaints followed, memoranda passed back and forth and mainly up toward the center, since, after all, the tasks of the plan had been set there.

Even simple problems, such as the ordering of a part to repair a machine, became bogged down in paperwork. Each producer was bound by tight monopoly ties to particular customers and suppliers and there was no alternative. The inflexibility of relationships, a feature of the old Stalinist model of centralized planning, itself became an obstacle to simple solutions. In a semi-market economy a manager is customarily able to consider alternative solutions to, for example, the problem of shortage of a particular material. In an overcentralized plan this becomes a problem which must await solution of some other problem elsewhere.

Problems which could be simply and easily solved at the lower level if plant managers had the authority, become real dilemmas when passed on up to the center. Then the top must decide everything—from a shortage of a particular size of bolt to questions of whether a plant should be closed. It becomes impossible to sort out and give attention to problems according to their social importance, or to know all the relevant facts required for a sensible decision. Once a decision is made it must pass down the hierarchy to the point of action—and by the time it reaches those who need the decision it may be far too late. The situation may have changed, or the delay have resulted in loss of production and further problems for other parts of the economy. It often becomes impossible to find out even who is responsible for the difficulty. Recriminations spoil normal relationships and the onrushing flow of memoranda, each with a new question for the center to decide, become overwhelming. Professor Parkinson, to the best of our knowledge, has not yet formulated a law covering this multiplication of problems once a centrally administered plan begins to break down.

In short, an overambitious, overcentralized plan can become a liability rather than an aid to management. It causes confusions because it sets up unrealistic expectations and yet upon those expectations depends the actual trend of incomes and the well-being of the entire society. Once an administrative plan begins to break down it becomes, in the extreme case, no plan at all. This was the strange situation in which Czechoslovakia found itself in 1962:

too much plan and in reality no plan. The only way out was to cut back on the volume of investments in new projects and, above all, to shift to labor-saving types of investment and away from extensive, labor-consuming projects.

This meant abandoning the Plan and, understandably, led to a belated attempt to discover the underlying causes of the difficulties. Once this examination got under way it became evident that the breakdown resulted from a whole complex of interrelated economic, political, and social factors. Each economist who has examined the data has tried to make them more meaningful by stressing a few main factors. For example, Ota Šik, who has had more intimate experience with planning than almost any one who has written about the Czechoslovak experience, became so convinced of the importance of erroneous and dogmatic theory that he started his book *Plan and Market Under Socialism,* with a long polemic against dogmatic thinking. The well-known Polish economist, W. Brus, lists five major factors as retarding growth: inflexibility of production; excessive inputs, particularly of materials; insufficient incentives for technological development; shortages and disharmonies within the system of stimuli and resulting alienation; and growth of bureaucracy. (Brus, *Modely socialistického hospodářství,* Prague, 1964, pp. 117–18.) Goldmann and Kouba concluded that: "Consequently, the downward trend in growth rate can only appear as the objective outcome of a single factor—the direct and indirect operation of the traditional (centralized) management system." (*Op. cit.,* p. 74.)

My own probing of the problem leads me back beyond the economic model itself to the political model, the misconception and abuse of the role of the "dictatorship of the proletariat" in the era of socialism. The difficulty with such generalizations is that they explain too much and so themselves require explanation. Therefore it seems unavoidable, if we are to understand the developments and problems in Czechoslovakia, that we make a rather broad selection of factors and then try to show how one development is linked with another, how solution of one problem awaits the solution of another, and why, in the end, we must experiment with both new theories and new practice. If socialism is to thrive and fructify to full advantage we cannot allow our theory to become dogmatic or our management to become bureaucratic.

Because there are many contradictions in the centralized and administrative model of planning and management and since their discussion will occupy a large part of this book, some readers may arrive at the conclusion that we think that the problems are insoluble and therefore that socialism is unworkable. This is not so. Modern society, and the technology with which it produces the commodities and services which we demand, has become so social in character that effective mechanisms must operate to protect the *social* interest. Some form of social planning and control is essential, and it seems clear that the social ownership of the means of production facilitates those social controls. Private ownership of the means of production, and production solely for profit in the market, leads with increasing frequency to contradictions requiring government interventions. Too often these interventions come belatedly, and serious, even irreparable damage is done to our living environment. Also, and too often, a mixture of socialism with capitalism takes on the undesirable features of both and results in partial and makeshift arrangements.

Market Competition and Central Planning

Before we discuss the merits of the market, even imperfect forms of it, let us be perfectly clear that the action of the market alone is no "invisible hand" leading to optimum social welfare. Consumer demand, left unchecked, can lead the economy and society far astray and create gigantic economic, social, and moral problems that in the end require solution by non-market-oriented decisions. For this reason all societies limit some forms of market choice—for example, none permits the free sale of narcotics. And what is narcotic? Will society be able to control the health hazards resulting from the market demand for cigarettes? What about the automobile and the fact that in the United States, where that industry has matured, the resulting problems of decay of city centers, pollution of the air—even the disposal of the old car bodies themselves—all have become acute and require *social* controls, social planning, and social intervention? Or consider the effect of market-oriented television upon culture! No, the market *alone* is no panacea. But it also cannot be ignored completely as the Stalinist model planners thought.

Today we find that many economists whose main experience has been with capitalist economies are denigrating the market and arguing that planning must be substituted for it. Economists who have worked in centrally planned economies that have been making little use of the market are, in contrast, urging that a larger role be assigned to the market. Of course we find no unanimity of opinion about the market among economists of either capitalist or socialist countries.

The recognition that the market is a far from perfect instrument for allocating resources and distributing incomes is as old as the monopoly efforts to manipulate the market and control prices. One of the most persuasive of the recent advocates of planning as opposed to the market is Professor John Kenneth Galbraith who argues:

> From the time and capital that must be committed, the inflexibility of this commitment, the needs of large organization and the problems of market performance under conditions of advanced technology comes the necessity for planning. The more sophisticated the technology, the greater, in general, will be the foregoing requirements. . . .
> In addition to deciding what the consumer will want and will pay, the firm must take every feasible step to see that what it decides to produce is wanted by the consumer at a remunerative price. And it must see that the labor, materials and equipment that it needs will be available at a cost consistent with the price it will receive. It must exercise control over what is sold. It must exercise control over what is supplied. It must replace the market with planning.
> (Galbraith, *The New Industrial State*, Houghton Mifflin, Boston, 1967, pp. 15–16 and 23–24.)

This is a statement of what every large corporation would like to be able to do, but even giants such as General Motors succeed only partly in doing. Even a cursory examination of the fluctuations in sales of automobiles can demonstrate that the corporate planners do not have anything like perfect "market control," yet they can make effective plans for development and can operate at high rates of efficiency and profit. Galbraith also develops the old theme that advancing technology has separated management from ownership.[6] In Galbraith's term these managers form a "techno-

---
[6] For earlier expressions of these ideas see A. Berle and G. Means, *The Modern Corporation and Private Property*, 1934, and James Burnham, *The Managerial Revolution*, 1941.

structure" and are not motivated by profit: "Profit maximization, as we have just seen, is inconsistent with the behavior of the technostructure." (*Ibid.,* p. 129.) One might think that this would lead Galbraith to conclude that since capitalists no longer managed their property, some form of social ownership would be appropriate. Instead he contends that "In nearly all the non-communist world socialism meaning public ownership of industrial enterprises, is a spent slogan." (p. 104.)

Curiously, except that they argue that planning will work only with social ownership, the supporters of the old Stalinist concept of centralized planning without the market have much in common with Galbraith. We can take as an example of this an article by two German Democratic Republic economists, Wolfgang Berger and Otto Reinhold. They wrote:

> As we see it, if the problems of the plan and market were linked, mistakes would be bound to occur. The market is a definite set of economic processes, whereas the plan is an expression of a subjective will.
>
> (*World Marxist Review,* July 1968, p. 29.)

But, after stating that the plan is based on subjective judgment and will, Berger and Reinhold make the contention that planning is a process of recognizing and using "definite objective laws" and that

> after resolving antagonistic class contradictions and removing the machinery of capitalist competition, we can make use of these laws for the public good. What it boils down to is that we can run the economic processes consciously, according to the plan, by virtue of our knowledge of objective laws.
>
> (*Ibid.,* p. 30.)

It turns out, however, that what these authors mean by "recognizing and using objective laws" is market research:

> It stands to reason that we in the GDR analyze the demand as accurately as we can and produce relevant forecasts as the basis for planning. (p. 30.)

They conclude:

> While some economists hold that the market alone makes truly scientific planning possible, we believe (and it can be proved)

that scientific planning should be based on the objective socialist laws operating in all spheres of the reproduction process. (p. 32.)

But how can planners use the "law of value" if prices of commodities are fixed centrally on a subjective basis?

Much of this talk about objective laws has been self-deception and served as a cover to protect the policies and decisions of the planners. One of the most popular of all the "laws" in the 1950's was "The law of planned proportional development." Just what this meant, *and how it could be an economic law acting independently of human will,* was never clearly explained.[7] Yet because it was asserted so vigorously many people were convinced that the plan was necessarily the optimum one for harmonious development of their country.

It was only when this claim for "proportional development" ran aground on the hard rocks of economic disequilibrium, such as the crisis of the plan in Czechoslovakia in 1962–63, that confidence in, and reliance on, these "laws" began to give way to scientific analysis. This reevaluation of economic theory and practice has been going on among the economists of all the socialist countries, although some are much further along in their analysis than others. In Czechoslovakia a good share of the pioneering work was done by Ota Šik who summarizes his argument as follows:

> The basis for a transition to intensive[8] growth in the present situation is to carry out basic structural changes in production, to assure a genuine, qualitative development of production factors.
>
> A basic prerequisite for this is doing away with the system of administrative planned management which had caused a loss of perspective because of the instability of the long-range plans and also determined production by one-sided, mainly quantitative and uneconomic orientation of activities and incentives. It led to quite unnecessary investments and needlessly expensive growth of production; needless consumption of material; an avoidance of technical and qualitative development; growing disproportions, or a continual state of emergency and shortages; a lag of

---
[7] Some economists try to argue that socialist economic laws are "consciously enforced." That means that they are not laws, but goals—which is quite another matter.
[8] Šik means capital-intensive, labor-saving investments.

services, science and research, and in the educational system; retarded the rise in consumption and leveled wage and salary scales, which again slowed down qualitative development.

But, especially, the administrative system of management restricted the independence of the enterprise and undermined the optimum development of their initiative. . . . Changing over to genuinely planned management and a consistent use of socialist market relationships is a condition for a lasting improvement in a socialist economy.

(Ota Šik, *Plan and Market Under Socialism,* Akademia, Prague, 1967, pp. 97–98.)

Šik, unlike Berger and Reinhold, argues from long experience with centralized planning that centralized planners cannot know the real costs of a product and therefore cannot "apply the law of value" unless those values are tested in a competitive market:

To assure the reproduction process . . . value is still a necessity, showing by commodity exchange if the labor expended is socially necessary.
(*Ibid.,* p. 226.)

An article by P. Krylov at the end of 1968 indicates that the Soviet Union is hesitantly moving not only toward some decentralization of planning, but also is experimenting with use of the market:

The economic reform now under way in the USSR presupposes the correct combination of single nation-wide planning with wider independence and initiative of enterprises and a higher role of republican and local economic planning and economic agencies. . . .

Elimination of the existing disproportions in the development of some branches, establishment of a dependable balance between them, is an economic precondition of correct definition of the sphere of centralized planning. A number of branches of mining still lag behind manufacturing industries, the production of consumer goods still lags behind the increase in incomes of the population, there are still difficulties in providing manpower for the national economy, etc. . . .

The State Committee for Material and Technical Supply is conducting an experiment in unlimited sale of separate items from

centralized state resources in a number of regions. . . . Evidently the time had come for a thorough elaboration of a general program of changing the system of planned material and technical supply in keeping with the demands of the economic reform.
(P. Krylov, "Problems of Improving Centralized Planning," *Planovoye Khozyaistvo*, No. 12, 1968.)

At the operating level and among those directly concerned with problems of planning we find now a deep concern with the disproportions that have developed under centralized planning. Ironically, prevention of such disproportions was long assumed to be one of the main advantages of centralized planning. Experience of the last decade shows that centralized planning without the market cannot prevent the growth of disproportions. How to create an effective socialist market to assist in guiding the development of the central plan will be a major task in the next years.

Competition and Change

Since at least at this stage of technological and social development, a healthy society requires constant change, one line of inquiry is to examine all of the factors which promote or retard change, for better or for worse, and the means of controlling those changes. Capitalism had an advantage over previous forms of production relations in that it freed entrepreneurs from many of the monopoly restraints of feudalism. Market competition developed and this became the mechanism upon which the profit and growth of the enterprise depended—and it was at the same time the mechanism which exerted ruthless pressure on the less efficient or less fortunate. Poverty and bankruptcy soon overtook those who would not or could not change. In this system there was at first no need for an elaborate hierarchy of decision-making. The entrepreneur estimated what would bring a profit in the market and bought the materials and invested in the plant to produce it. If he miscalculated it was his loss—and that of his workers. There was a premium on fast, direct decisions and upon efficiency of the entire operation. These pressures operated also on the workers—no one can deny that capitalism can be very efficient in exploiting its workers. Here we are not concerned with all of the defects inherent in capitalism which led, among other things, to increasing impairment of the market as an efficient means of allocating resources.

What we are concerned with at this point is that the market and competition were highly effective mechanisms for promoting change. But the very pressures that made that competition work —for example, the threat of loss of capital or of a job or of a farm —were so brutal and so much hated that one of the goals of socialism became that of reducing competition and substituting security. In purusit of this security, and of efficient use of resources and economies of scale, socialist planners have as a matter of course promoted monopoly more complete than anything possible under capitalism even with international cartels. Of course it was a different kind of monopoly and was intended to serve social rather than private purposes. Nevertheless that monopoly concept, permeating all society, has very seriously retarded scientific thinking and the introduction of technological innovation into the production process.

In virtually eliminating market competition, socialism in the early period did make many immediate gains, as we have noted, for example, in avoiding some duplications and idle plant capacity.[9] But it has paid a high price for this, and a price that in many ways is mounting year by year. In the end we will find this decline of competition to be an important element in nearly all problems, whether that of innovation in technology, quality of product, work morale, or even problems outside the sphere of economics, in politics and cultural life. In fact, fear of competition in ideas became an obsession with those who held the reins of power. This, ultimately, may prove to be the greatest defect of the old Stalinist model of socialism.

A market cannot function unless there is enough pressure on producers to force them to alter, to conform to demand, their prices and volume as well as type of production. Those who criticize, correctly, the rigidity of long-term planning and hope for the flexibility of the market, must realize that there can be no flexible response without effective competition. And that means inevitably some reserves of productive capacity, some idle resources. How to get the advantages of competitive pressures for change and yet avoid the losses (and in the case of unemployment, suffering) of unused resources will be one of the most difficult problems of the

---

[9] Later much idle capacity was developed and in some industries a very large amount of duplication. For example, some 240 plants in Czechoslovakia make ball bearings!

future. A socialist country that for years has promoted administrative monopoly cannot hope to wave a wand and introduce an effective market. There will be strong vested interests against the reintroduction of effective competition, a strong demand for the efficiencies of large-scale production—and in a small country such as Czechoslovakia even one producer may be able to saturate the market before attaining the full economies of large run-throughs.

How, then, can we be sure of having effective competition? Market competition cannot be effective unless changes in demand are reflected promptly in changes in prices and unless those prices (with carefully determined exceptions such as for medical care) reflect both socially necessary costs and quality. If the central administrative power insists upon setting all, or even most, of the prices in the wholesale and retail market it at the same time obstructs the operation of the market and restricts the gains from competition. In all advanced societies the government intervenes in the "market" to set prices of some products or services, such as rail transport, which are regarded as too important to tolerate monopoly pricing. The history of such regulation shows that it is very complex and difficult to administer both for political and for economic reasons. In the end, such regulation tends to break down, partly because it fosters bureaucracy and stagnation in the regulated industry, and also because the regulated monopoly tends to acquire the political power to turn the regulation in its favor and against the society on whose behalf the regulation was originally undertaken. (See the study of such transport problems in the United States by George S. Wheeler, *Kapitalismus a doprava* [Capitalism and Transport], Akademia, Prague, 1965.)

The difficulties experienced by capitalism in fixing monopoly prices should be studied carefully by socialist planners since they illustrate many of the problems inherent in all such attempts. One of these is the increasing difficulty which the price-setting agency has of knowing what real costs are and therefore what is a "fair" rate of return on capital, or a "fair" price socially. Socialism can mitigate some of the problems of price setting, particularly group pressures, by social ownership of the productive capacity. But it cannot avoid (and probably should not be able to avoid) those group pressures completely—the workers on the railways must be heard, for example, before fixing freight rates.

But it is significant that, despite all the difficulties of regulation of these types of monopolies and of arriving at proper prices for their goods and services, capitalist price setting continues. And socialism, with its greater concern for social interests, will certainly also have to continue with centrally fixed prices for some commodities and services. The socialist planners will undoubtedly find, as the regulators of capitalist monopolies have, that one of the most effective methods of price regulation is to undermine the monopoly position of the regulated enterprises. This may require direct government action to promote that competition, as when the United States Government built inland waterways so that barge transport competed with the railroads. The railroad managements protested furiously, but in the end they were forced to introduce technological innovations, such as 90-ton freight cars, which greatly improved efficiency and reduced costs. The capitalists persistently seek the security of monopoly, but in the end it is competition that forces them to make the technological innovation which gives the system its main strength and, ultimately, its only security.

This role of competition in forcing innovation cannot be ignored by socialist planners. On the contrary, market competition can be and often must be deliberately introduced both in the market for producers goods and for the retail market. For example, the Czechoslovak producers of home refrigerators persisted in making unchanged and obsolete models. The government imported from Egypt models that were so obviously superior that the people were willing to pay premium prices for them. Under the new system of management this reduced sales of the domestic producers and so put pressure on them to improve the quality of their refrigerators. A similar result was obtained in the import of other consumer commodities, such as radios and television sets.

In the installation of machine tools and electronic equipment it is often necessary to go beyond the socialist market to get the latest technology. It is clear that in some cases it is not economical or even possible for a small socialist country to undertake the costs of developing many types of equipment. In such cases the purchasing enterprise should be able (within the limits of social control of major investments) to buy the license or the machines for the most effective technology even if it means trade with the capitalist countries. This is sometimes a stimulation of competition, sometimes a recognition that specialization must in particular cases replace competition.

Encouragement of Quantity Rather than Quality

The old system of administrative monopoly, which tied customers to particular producers and allocated raw materials and all other essentials of production, precluded competition. If materials or machines were unsatisfactory the using enterprise (or the final consumer) had no real alternative. They used the obsolete or defective material and passed on in their own products the resulting lower quality. In acting in this manner they took the easy way—in some cases the only way—out of a production problem. It was the easy way out because, under the old system of centralized determination of the plan and the allocation of output targets down to the producing unit, the goal of production became the output of a specified number of units of a particular commodity. This system put a premium on standardization rather than innovation. Any attempts to specify quality necessarily had to be in terms of commodities and qualities being produced at the time the plan was being prepared, and that was, at the minimum, months and often years before the product was actually produced. In an industry with rapid innovation, such as electronics, it is not even possible to know five years in advance what products will be produced and in demand, let alone specify the quality of the product in such terms that quality can be suitably rewarded—suitably meaning rewarded well enough to encourage it, yet at prices that do not reward monopoly power in the market.

One might expect that socially minded managers would innovate in quality and introduce new products even though the long-term and centrally fixed prices did not themselves encourage such innovation. But it was extremely dangerous to innovate in the face of a rigid plan specifying given volumes of a commodity. The bonuses and premiums of the managers and engineers, and (to a certain extent) of the workers, depended upon producing at least the minimum number of units of the plan. If the enterprise fell short, even by a few units, the penalty was drastic. Often, in the periodic rush to meet the target of the plan, parts or products known to be defective were passed on in the hope that the lower quality would not be detected, or if so, tolerated.

This premium which centrally fixed targets placed upon quantity was not an occasional and accidental aberration. It appeared in all countries with the centralized administrative model of planning and management, and it persisted over long periods. Even after the introduction of the "new system" of management we find that not only do some managers still hesitate to innovate in terms of quality and new products, but when they do so, the supervising layer of bureaucrats may even forbid the innovation if it interferes with the production of the *quantity* specified in the plan.

A convenient example of this was the case of the Rosa Luxemburg knitting mill in Kiev, U.S.S.R. After having been put on the "new system" the factory director, Z. Belozerova, wanted to respond to the market demand by shifting over to new-type elastic kapron stockings—a shift which would have resulted in a profit of 10 million rubles to the state. But the *number* of pairs of stockings produced would have been only 3,900,000 instead of the 4,500,000 pairs of inferior quality cotton stockings called for in the centrally determined plan. The management was told by the higher organizations: "You have no right to make the change." (*Ekonomicheskaia Gazeta,* Moscow, No. 37, September 1967.)

Almost always a technological advance, whether to introduce a better quality product or to install a new piece of more productive equipment, entails a halt in the flow of production and a temporary loss in number of units produced. How long the delay will last is not certain since in any new technology entirely unexpected "bugs" may develop. If the plan specifies only the quantity to be turned out (and even that is almost impossible to do with more than a million items to be produced in a moderately developed economy), and success depends upon meeting at least that level of output, this is what the manager will normally choose to do. Since no immediate group rewards, and perhaps great risks, are attached to even simple changes, the intelligent form of *group* policy is to minimize risk and that means to minimize change and to hold back on all innovation. (This, too, is a subject to which we are led back many times.)

The specification of the plan in terms of tons of output may result not only in a distortion of output in favor of heavier parts, it may also be directly contrary to the main trend required by progressive technology. An engineer in the Vítkovice plant in Ostrava, Moravia, told me of his dilemma in designing giant walking earth movers. The world market has as one of its main tests the capacity of the earth mover in cubic meters of earth per hour in relation to the weight of the machine per square centimeter on its "feet." The lighter the pressure on the feet the more mobile the machine can be on soft ground. Yet fulfillment of the plan was in number of tons because that was the most convenient common denominator for the variety of heavy products turned out by the enterprise. In this case the scientific and social spirit of the engineer prevailed and he remarked with pride that his earth mover was the lightest in relation to capacity of any in the world. But a society cannot expect that its engineers and managers will be able and willing to innovate even at the risk of not fulfilling the plan.

Plant directors generally recognize the right and need for the central bodies to determine the general direction of social development and, in order to attain that end, the necessity to determine the main lines of investment and production. But they are also equally certain that the central administration does not know and *cannot know* the future trend of demand for all specific products, particularly new products. Again, if the center tries to specify *all* the lines and range of products, it inevitably hinders innovation. This is a constant factor in any country with a complex range of products such as Czechoslovakia—but again let us document the point with a recent discussion of factory directors in the Ukraine. There the meeting was reminded of a decision of October 4, 1965, by the Council of Ministers of the U.S.S.R., which stated that the enterprises were to solve independently the problems of production, bearing in mind the main tasks set by the plan. Instead of heeding this decision the central agencies persisted in the most detailed planning "down to the last screw."

V. Momet, director of a chemical enterprise, remarked:

> The entire range of products in our enterprise is planned at the top by the State Planning Board (GOSPLAN) and by the Union Republic Ministry. . . . At each step we feel that these organizations do not know the need of the consumers of our products well enough. This has a negative influence on the work of our enterprise.
>
> I shall give you an example. We received from our main directorship *(glavnoie upravleniie)* a letter referring to an order of the Ministry of Chemical Production of the USSR forbidding any overfulfillment of the plan of production of one of the herbicides. This chemical was supposed to have limited market possibilities. The same order said that overproduction of this herbi-

cide could not be taken into account in calculating the premium fund.

After this we received another order from the Ministry of the production of specified fertilizers and chemicals for the protection of plants—and this same herbicide was included among the chemicals urgently needed. A special premium was given for every ton of overfulfillment of the plan! And this, of course, was correct. We got lots of letters, and the heads of collectives and state farms visit us saying: "Supply us with this product, it was not assigned from above."

This was only one of the numerous examples given in the discussion. The problem lies not only in the fact that the planning organs do not know the demand for a given chemical product well enough; there are millions of sorts of products in our national economy, and *it is hopeless to try to plan all of them from above, even with the use of modern computers.*

(*Ekonomicheskaia Gazeta,* September 1967, No. 37. My emphasis. G.W.)

Here we find the sober conclusion, backed by long years of experience, that a central agency simply *cannot know in detail* the needs of the increasingly complex economy. And, as in this case, it cannot even be sure that its policies and directives in such an important productive input as herbicides are consistent and wise. It seems clear that in such cases the new chemical should be tested by some social agency to make sure that it does not have harmful residues, then to see that the product is made known in honest manner to the users. After that it should be up to the users to place their orders and the producers to respond to them. Even the prices could be set by local negotiation—with the possibility of appeal to higher bodies if the customers thought that the producer was charging a monopoly price.

Central Price Fixing Inhibits Change

Let us pursue the examination of the manner in which the old model of planning inhibited change. One assumption of the Stalinist model was that socialist planning eliminated commodities and the market and, as a corollary, that prices of practically all goods should be set socially and reflect social policy. One consequence of this, the divorce of prices from costs and value, and the resulting policy chaos, has been thoroughly examined by socialist economists, including Ota Šik in his previously cited book.[10] Here we take up the point that such centrally fixed prices necessarily tend to inhibit innovation. Central determination of prices involves such laborious calculations and adjustments that some prices have been unchanged in some countries for a decade or more—even if in the meantime there have been substantial changes in the internal or world costs of producing the item. Long-term fixing of prices in these cases gives the planners an easier way of making apparently satisfactory balances. It is true that these balances are illusory and conceal divergent real trends of social costs, but it may be a long time before these contradictions come to the surface.

What is more significant about the long-term and centrally fixed prices is that they tend to protect the users of obsolete equipment and the producers of obsolete products from the effects of both internal and external competition. In the world market an innovation may improve quality and make possible production at the same cost, or it may reduce costs for the same quality. In either case, if the producer is to continue to meet the market competition he must improve quality or reduce prices. But in the socialist countries with the state monopoly of foreign trade the enterprises do not have to worry about such forced changes. The long-run price insulates the manager from the need to change. He can meet the plan by an extensive development of his plant rather than by risking technical improvements in capacity or quality.

Some may protest that this is not the way "socialist man" *should* act. The answer is that this is the way he *does* act, given the directives of a central plan which has as its main target a stated amount or value of product. We do not need to argue about this: it has been the experience in small countries, such as Czechoslovakia, and in a giant one such as the Soviet Union. Its effects persist even in the initial stages of introduction of some elements of a "new system" of management, as we can see from the following discussion by V. Sitnin, Chairman of the State Committee on Prices of the U.S.S.R. State Planning Committee:

---

[10] This is one reason why Oscar Lange as early as 1957 concluded: "Prices should above all reflect the social production costs of the given product." Quoted in W. E. Griffith, *Communism in Europe*, M.I.T. Press, 1964, p. 165.

The wholesale price reform of July 1, 1967 is an important step in the establishment of the new system of management. . . . In working out the new price lists we sought to promote technical progress, higher quality of products and expansion of goods in short supply. . . .

Partial revision of prices should above all eliminate at the proper time the increased profitability of obsolete products and of products that are becoming obsolete. This will economically encourage the enterprises to introduce into production technically improved items and to use advanced techniques. To this end it is necessary to establish favorable prices for advanced equipment and "fines" for obsolescent equipment, that is, higher prices for new technically advanced products and reduced prices for products of obsolete design. . . .

In this connection we are confronted with an important problem: development of a price-regulating mechanism and establishment of the level of return of outdated products. If as a result of lower production costs the rate of return on outdated products shows a steady increase—the return on the new equipment should be higher than on that of the old equipment since otherwise the manufacturer will have no incentive—the costs tor machinery and other implements of labor will inevitably tend to grow. Such a relation would create an artificial barrier to the introduction of new equipment.

Timely revision of prices of old equipment [and of consumer goods?—G.W.] will be best insured by mobile prices. . . .

However, this will be possible only if the technicians in the ministries, enterprises and design organizations take part in working out mobile prices together with the economists. This will enable them correctly to establish the time when the products become morally obsolete. . . . The introduction of such methods will mark the transition of price formation practices to a qualitatively higher stage. But before this step can be made, complex methodological problems will have to be solved. . . . Shortcomings in bookkeeping smother the incentives to put out better products which offer a higher profit level. Inadequate recording of costs creates additional difficulties in determining the true economic effect of the introduction of new equipment. Calculation of production costs should be in the spotlight of the attention of the executive and production personnel of the enterprise. (*Ekonomicheskaia Gazeta,* No. 47, 1968.)

We regret not being able to quote in full this article by the Chairman of the State Committee on Prices of the country with the longest experience with centralized planning and price fixing. It shows that top-level Soviet planners are fully aware that the existing (1968) system of fixing prices does not offer adequate incentives either to improve quality or to introduce new technology. At the time Sitnin made his speech some prices had been revised 14 months earlier, but mainly on the basis of information dating back to 1965—and he urged immediate attention to the problem in order to be able to introduce new wholesale prices by January 1970. Even so, these price changes would involve only a small part of the total—for example, about 2,500 engineering products. In practice, some wholesale prices have been in effect for as long as a decade.

Most significant is that the *method* of revising prices proposed by Sitnin is far too cumbersome to be effective, and, in the end, the economists, ministries, enterprises, and design organizations would have no effective way of knowing whether and to what degree a product was "morally obsolete" *except by comparison of its qualities with similar products in the world market.*[11] Some useful information could be had by the response of users in the internal market, but since the consumers in that market would be comparing the new and the old products on the basis of subjectively and centrally established prices which do not reflect socially necessary costs, the action of the internal market would yield only partial information.

We fully agree with Sitnin that under the system in which fulfilling plan targets is the main task "the manufacturing enterprises seek to retain excessively high prices, because they fear that they might fail to fulfill the plan. This situation must be rectified at once." *(Ibid.)* In short, the method of centrally setting prices not only retards innovation and furnishes inadequate incentives for quality; it also, when combined with centrally set plan targets for the enterprises, puts a premium upon exaggeration by the enter-

---

[11] Since its second meeting in 1949 the socialist countries in COMECON have used world market prices as the basis for calculating their own commodity transactions, with adjustments for transport costs.

prise of its costs in an effort to keep up the prices allowed to it. Here in one article we have the admission by the Chairman of the Soviet State Price Committee that the centralized administrative pricing mechanism has not performed some of its most important functions, and that no effective system has yet been worked out by which prices can attain the flexibility needed to put a premium upon innovation, quality and *efficiency*.

In their study of this situation the Czechoslovak economists reached the conclusion that it was not possible for administrators to set prices centrally for all of the vast assortment of commodities produced in the country in a manner that would encourage innovation and quickly reflect the effects of new levels of "socially necessary costs." In fact, a decentralization of the price-fixing function becomes more imperative as the economy comes to produce an increasing variety of goods and as scientific-technological changes occur with increasing frequency. No single central agency could possibly cope with the problem of *timely* price changes for such a vast range of goods. It cannot, as the Sitnin quotation shows, avoid a very serious lag in time of the price changes, and this consistently rewards bad quality and obsolete methods of production.

The question is how to get prices that *stimulate* innovation. Nearly all economists in Czechoslovakia are convinced that centralized setting of some prices is essential to protect the social interest, but that all other prices must be arrived at on a decentralized basis. The power to adjust prices must be decentralized to an enterprise level or to some other local basis, probably with price limits for some relatively important commodities. Free adjustment of some other prices, mainly of nonessential consumer goods and services, to meet market conditions could be permitted. This would greatly reduce the number of commodities for which prices needed to be centrally fixed and permit the price-fixing agencies to act more promptly in regard to the prices of more important products and services.

One of the more important functions of the market under socialism would be this reduction of the administrative burden in pricing and in increasing the flexibility of pricing generally. As I have said, without competitive pressures the rate of innovation is certain to lag, and there can be no effective pressures (as distinct from exhortation) without a market, and no market without prices that respond to changes in real costs of production.[12] The market serves other functions which we will later consider, but here I should point out that not only can it reduce to a tolerable level the administrative burden (and related bureaucracy) of price setting, but also reduce the administrative load of attempting to determine the *quantities* of many hundreds of thousands of products and the *qualities* that are more socially desirable. If some central agency insists on attempting to make all these decisions, even if equipped with the latest information-processing technology, it will inevitably find itself so overburdened with detail that it will be able to perform none of its functions satisfactorily. This is not a new argument. In essence it dates back to Adam Smith, but its validity had to be learned all over again by the experience of the last two decades with central administrative planning.[13] Here we have a major reason why some form of synthesis of central planning and a competitively active market must be worked out.

Necessity of Incentives for Change

In May 1968, N. Baibakov, Chairman of the U.S.S.R. State Planning Commission, said:

> We must consider and discuss some problems connected with the economic stimulation of engineering progress....
>
> Indeed, we know, for example, of a number of cases when in some articles scarce materials are rightly and effectively replaced by less scarce and cheaper materials, and this led to a lessening of volume of realized output and, hence, to a lessening

---

[12] The reader may think from this that the author has read neither Schumpeter on innovation and monopoly nor Galbraith on the obsolescence of the market. He has, but despite elements of truth in the able arguments of each, thinks that his own interpretation is the one that will prevail in economies with complex and large-scale production.

[13] For manufacturing alone the Central Economico-Mathematical Institute, U.S.S.R. Academy of Sciences, has made the following approximate calculations: There are some 50,000 medium and large factories in the Soviet Union manufacturing more than two million types of products and using more than one million types of raw materials and semifinished materials and other resources. A plan model will contain more than two million variables and one million equations. To calculate even one version of a plan would require 10^{18} arithmetic operations. A computer performing one million operations per second would require about 30,000 years to complete one plan. (*Rabochi Klass i Sovremenny Mir*, No. 5–6, 1971.)

of profits that go into the fund of material stimulation. However, these shortcomings are easily eradicable.

It should be stressed that the potentialities of the new methods of economic management and the system of stimulation of technical progress have far from been exhausted. This concerns the planning of technical progress, price formation and the utilization of the profit and loss accounting funds. The reform helps not only to reconsider the conservative approach to technical policies, but also creates sound economic prerequisites for the introduction of new machinery.

(*Ekonomicheskaia Gazeta,* No. 21, May 1968.)

Chairman Baibakov argues that the "new system" of management is better suited than the old when it comes to stimulating change. But I am not so sure that the existing difficulties can be "easily eradicated." That depends on many factors, and on what is meant by the "new system." If the new system continues to require fulfilment of the plan in terms of quantity or value, it is certain that innovation, as under the old system, is very risky since all bonuses may be lost by some unexpected difficulty which temporarily reduces output.[14]

How much risk a manager and his immediate staff are willing to take depends also on the rewards which are allowed for such "entrepreneurship." That again depends on a great many factors such as how different the new method is, the costs of the new technology as compared to the old, the quality of the product, and, if it is improved, if the prices are promptly adjusted to reward the better quality. As we have just seen, such price adjustments are not so easy or automatic under centralized price setting. But equally important is the tax system. If all, or all but an insignificant part, of the "profits" from innovation are promptly taxed away into the

---

[14] As recently as March 1969 a factory manager in Latvia complained that they were not permitted to use a new plastic in transistors. It is difficult to change established habits of bureaucratic management, particularly if the reform is partial as it has been so far in the U.S.S.R. There the right to pay premiums or bonuses depends not on market sales but on plan fulfillment, and so enterprises still tend to submit low plans and hesitate to innovate for fear that an interruption in production might deprive them of the right to use funds for incentives even though other indicators, such as increase in productivity, had been met. Many enterprises are required to buy from and sell to other specific firms and this prevents any effective market pressures on costs and prices. (*Rudé právo,* March 11, 1969.)

central budget, the enterprise managers will certainly tend to be conservative in their estimates of the usefulness of the new technology. It may be that society has been primarily responsible for the scientific or technical progress, and in that case society should get *most* of the gain from increased productivity. But unless a substantial gain is apparent for both the managers *and the workers,* and unless this gain is fairly secure over a period of time, both workers and managers will resist innovation. There is a long history of experience in Czechoslovakia to support this statement—and it cannot be assumed that the workers there are any less socially minded than in other socialist countries.

Most technicians, engineers, and workers have a natural interest in doing their jobs in a better way and in innovation, but relatively few will persist in offering innovations if the management makes it difficult or risky. Care must be taken that each person is given proper share in the credit for the idea and that the rewards have some relation to the social value of the change. For instance, a worker may have an "improvement suggestion" for which he may get 500 crowns, often less. Later he will see some engineer develop the idea and get a much bigger reward, and finally the director of the plant will be decorated for the fine results of the suggestion. In the best Czechoslovak plants this difficulty has been partly overcome by making team awards. But in many other plants under mediocre management credit is stolen, or more often the idea is ignored. The easy thing to do was to increase the amount of the wage fund by increasing the number of workers upon which for many years the amount of the wage fund depended. For a bureaucratic-minded manager this was much the safer way, and one he could understand. Under this system a redundant number of workers, not new technology, was the key to plan fulfillment.

In all socialist countries lip service is paid to the goal of equalization of incomes. Yet only Czechoslovakia put into practice such a narrow range of incomes. A large factory which I visited in 1969 had a lower level of wages of 1,100 crowns a month, average wages of about 1,680 crowns, and a top income for the director of 3,000 crowns. The director did have some fringe benefits, such as a car. But it is not unusual to find in a plant that many of the top men among the engineers and at lower levels of management were actually paid less than some of the skilled workers. A foreman, for example, might earn less than he could at the bench—and often he chose to avoid the responsibility and remain at the bench. This, eventually, became a serious problem and led to agitation among managers and intellectuals for higher income differentials—a move which the workers have so far resisted quite successfully. Generally they are not so opposed to higher pay for higher skills, but too often the higher pay went to political bureaucrats—and for these any pay was excessive.

It is in this equalitarian setting that we should consider the higher rewards for successful innovation—or just good management generally. Under the old system if a plant or a cooperative farm or a shop consistently overfulfilled its plan it was given a stiffer plan the next time. If a shop, by good salesmanship, sold more than the plan it got a bonus, and perhaps even a special award. Then next year its plan was increased and it was expected to sell more before bonus payment began. If a cooperative produced more by better methods of farming, it could find that extra earnings had been drained away in differential taxes, reclassification of its land, or some other device which bureaucrats became expert in devising.

It cannot be said that this was exactly the same as the "speed-up" of capitalism because the benefits of the higher tempo of work or of the higher planned output are social and do not go to the profit of property owners. But to the individuals or groups immediately involved, the higher norm of work was so much like the old speedup that they began to resist change also under socialism. It took only a few years of such experiences to harden the attitude of the workers against innovation, even though no loss of job was involved. Any innovation means loss of skill for *some* workers or the need to shift work-places, and in the end their wages would average about the same, in spite of the increased productivity, as those of workers in less efficient plants.

About ten years ago the surplus capacity for producing motorcycles was so great that some plants had to be closed. The Jawa plant in Prague was chosen for conversion to production of semiconductors. Many skilled workers who had been used to handling large parts could not adapt to the new work, but they also did not want to shift to work in their own trade in other plants in the city. In the end the plant conversion was made, and most of the workers are women who had not worked at Jawa. The transition here was much eased because in the same city were many alternative places to work. Closing an obsolete enterprise in a country area without other employment raises many political and social problems which are much more difficult to solve, yet which must be solved before the workers of the plant can be expected to cooperate in the change. In any event the policy of low rents and low investment in new housing meant that no vacant flats were available and so the work force was partly immobilized or frozen in the old locations of industry.

It should not be thought that workers and managers *always* resisted innovation that increased productivity, but they did so more often than is usually admitted; and in some cases went to extremes which would not be tolerated under capitalism—extremes which they could insist upon because of the power of the local trade unions and the difficulty of discharging recalcitrant workers. Let us take two typical examples of this from industry. Early in 1968 a packaging machine was imported and set up in a Prague factory. It had a rated capacity of 1,100 packages per hour. But the foreman told me that workers insisted that the machine could actually package only 900 per hour and refused to let it run faster. Furthermore they insisted that the machine run only 6 hours per day—and this despite the fact that there was a real shortage of the product being packaged!

When I related this incident to a fellow economist he said that the foreman was lucky to get the workers to man the machine at all. He had worked in a factory where the management had installed a new automatic lathe, but had neglected to consult with the union before bringing in the machine. Not one worker would man it, and after it had been idle for months it was actually removed and replaced with a lathe of the old type.

Such resistance to innovation at the level of operation is in direct contrast to the hopes held out for socialism as liberating the initiative of workers to increase production. It is this contrast between the dream and reality which has long intrigued and often baffled me. Let us examine some specific cases, each of which illustrates some weakness in the incentives for change.

One of the arguments that turned me toward socialism more than forty years ago was that monopolies held back on quality. The story then current was that Gillette had deliberately reduced the quality of razor blades so that after a few shaves one would have to use (and buy) a new one. "When we get socialism we will produce a really good blade." Instead, blades produced under socialist centralized administrative planning, where presumably quality of such a simple item could be specified, have been among the world's worst. Since I had good friends in the Czechoslovak industry I tried to find out why. All kinds of *excuses* were given, even that the quality of the ore available was not right. When I remonstrated that only a few tons of ore and less of steel would make all the blades Czechoslovakia could use in a year, the reasons shifted to improper finishing machines, etc.[15]

Then, after the new system was introduced rewarding the enterprise according to sales and not number of blades, a miracle occurred: The Czechs began producing a blade, "Astra," as good as any in the world! The enterprise bought an English patent and some machines, and the torture of outrageous quality blades was over. Why was this innovation not pioneered long ago by Czechoslovak industry? The answer is clear. There were no economic incentives to justify the risks involved in making the change or to stimulate the necessary managerial and engineering efforts. If that effort had been made two decades ago Czechoslovakia by now would have a fine export market for a product requiring only small inputs of resources.

In many seemingly small, but in total very important, ways socialist technology is still a full half a century behind the most advanced capitalist technology. Many of these small items (or even methods of work) would require only comparatively small investments to produce and no complicated technology. I have in mind such things as work tools, wrecking bars, mops and mop wringers, work clothes, work gloves, orchard and garden equipment, and dozens of labor-saving devices in the home such as egg beaters and can openers. Yes, I know that there is a Czech institute that turns out beautiful hand-fitting *models* of some special tools—but try and buy one!

At the time I started to do farm work more than fifty years ago we had good, light, three-legged ladders for orchard work such as fruit picking. When used with a picking bag for such hard fruit as apples or pears a man can pick about four or five times as much fruit per day as with the present equipment used in the socialist countries. Also the ladders are safer and damage the trees less. For

---

[15] The Klement Gottwald Steel Works in Ostrava actually did produce some fine sample blades in the late 1950s but none reached the market.

more than a decade I used this as a standard example of one reason why fruit in socialist countries is so costly—but I have yet to see any interest in the subject.[16]

My conclusion is that the central planners *can* have no interest in such seemingly trivial items—unless it somehow happens to become involved in "politics." About a decade ago a friend who styles clothing was admiring my blue denim work jacket and pants. I asked: "Why don't you produce them?" He said: "Look, it would take too much cotton." I protested that they outwore two sets of Czech work clothes and so would *save* cotton. No interest. Then the "hippies" found out that jeans are comfortable and they became a status symbol and a black-market item. At this point the protectors of socialist culture discovered jeans to be a "decadent bourgeois influence!" In one neighboring country long lectures were given on the subject by experts who did not even know that jeans first became standard work clothes in the United States about the time of the 1849 California gold rush. Now jeans are made in Czechoslovakia, and this may have been one thing that convinced some people that the Czechs and Slovaks had indeed gone too far. . . .

Confused politics does inhibit the introduction to the market of some items in high demand, but it is a relatively minor factor in explaining the lack of so many productively useful or just satisfying but small items. Such a widespread and persistent disregard of these "fringe" commodities is rooted in the centralized model of management of the economy. One explanation is that from sheer necessity the central planners simply cannot take time to consider and put into the plan these thousands of relatively less important commodities. It takes all the time of the planners to decide about the major trends of the economy, the extent of investment in relation to consumption, major projects such as the kind of power plant (whether atomic or not), location, size, etc. One 1,000-million-crown project must get prior consideration over dozens of proposals that add up to the same total investment. If considered at all, a small item (as Parkinson has pointed out), may take as much or more time as a major one.

The result is that central planners *cannot,* and the enterprises

---

[16] In high-wage countries ladders are themselves obsolete for such work, but with wage rates of the socialist countries they would pay for themselves in one season.

often do not, bother to include minor new products in the plan and, not being included, they cannot be produced. (Production of spare parts also is usually regarded as a nuisance.) No one's specific economic interest is involved to the extent that makes it worthwhile to go through all of the efforts, overcome all of the bureaucratic red tape and resistance, and accept all of the risks involved in putting a new product on the market—unless the item happens to be something that catches the interest of someone with political power.

There are several "solutions" for this problem (aside from the characteristic bureaucratic response of denying that it exists). In the socialist country with most success in producing and marketing such small-volume commodities, the German Democratic Republic, the problem has been neatly sidestepped by allowing *private* producers to make and sell such items outside the plan. If you look at the labels on such items in any shop in East Germany you will find a very high proportion of the range of commodities to have been produced by private enterprise. One estimate is that almost 30 percent of the *items* in retail trade were so produced.

The proportion of private manufacturing enterprises is even higher. In 1966, of a total of 13,451 industrial enterprises in the G.D.R. only 3,843 were socialist, while 5,512 were joint (with the share of private ownership ranging from 10 to 90 percent), and 4,096 were strictly private enterprises. The private and joint companies together formed 71.5 percent of the enterprises, employed 16.2 percent of workers, and produced 12.1 percent of the gross industrial product. The average number of employees of private firms was 24, but four had more than 200 workers. These proportions have been about the same since 1961. (German Democratic Republic, *Statistisches Jahrbuch,* 1967, pp. 113 and 136.) Not having to plan in detail the production of these thousands of small capitalist and part-capitalist firms relieved the central planners of a great burden of administrative work.

Economists in Czechoslovakia do not generally regard this as a desirable solution, and instead advocate a decentralization of planning and a change in its character so that not all these useful, but socially not vital, items would have to be centrally planned. Instead, public enterprises, and *particularly producer cooperatives,* should be encouraged to make such products, explore the market for them, set their prices, and produce the volume that the market will take. If a reasonable part of the net return were allowed to remain with the producers this would encourage them to produce many new commodities—at least those for which a demand is known to exist. Such enterprises need not be *privately* owned, but such small-scale production (and some small-scale services such as shoe repair) could even be private if no or few workers are hired. They should not be centrally planned. It is enough that the central planners know approximately the volume of manpower and materials that will be required. Otherwise the cooperatives and local publicly owned producers and servicers should be subject to a very minimum of controls.

If bureaucracy is allowed to take charge of such services as housecleaning, they are sure to work up such a maze of paperwork that most of the charges for the service go to the bureaucrats and not to the workers performing the service. This is not theory, but experience. Some time ago it was announced in Prague that a new service had been set up to relieve the overworked housewife: a complete housecleaning service, "Úklid." We tried it and, being amazed at the size of the bill, figured out that only *one half* of the amount was for wages (including social security) and materials such as soaps and polishes. The rest went for taxes and new echelons of bureaucrats. That way, obviously, will not help the low-income woman who needs such assistance. Perhaps, small *competing* service cooperatives, or individuals working on their own, would help. Only experimentation under socialist conditions, but without the costs of bureaucratic monopoly "supervision," can assure a solution.

We have explored some of the difficulties of attaining innovation in small-scale operations first because it is easier to see the problems and perhaps even where the solutions may be found. The problems are similar but far more fundamental in heavy industry and in large-scale productive activities because generally it is here that most production occurs. Here it is not just a question of frequent lag in adoption of long-known techniques, but of the lack of initiative in new technology as well as slowness in developing many industries. There are exceptions, important ones, such as in the geological exploration for oil or the generation of electric power. In Czechoslovakia major breakthroughs in textile manufacturing were made with shuttleless weaving and spindleless spinning. These must be studied to see why they are exceptionally successful. Usually, but not always, they are defense-related industries to which the planners have attached particular importance, allowed generous funds, and minimized the restrictions on scientists and engineers who are put in charge of research and development.

In other industries, including basic services such as transport, there have been economies of scale and many correct decisions, such as to electrify the main lines of the railways, and to develop public transport as a priority over private automobiles. But generally there has been far more *discussion* of scientific technology, such as electronics and automation, miniaturization and new materials such as plastics and rare metals, than its actual application in production. The lag in *use* of numerical- or tape-controlled machinery, or the slowness in developing efficient atomic power plants, are examples of this. It is not that the planners and engineers are unaware of what they should be doing, as any visit to the International Trade Fair at Brno can confirm. The great gap is between known technology and its use. That depends upon the kind of machinery and equipment *produced,* as well as upon the incentives for its introduction into the various industries.

Several years ago one of the editors of a Prague journal called me and said: "You have been talking for a long time about the need for new labor-saving machinery for agriculture. This morning's *Rudé právo* has a big story that the agricultural machine plant at Roudnice has developed six machines of just the type we need, a new potato harvester, potato and sugar beet planters and rotary hoes. If I make the appointment and send a car and photographer would you go and write it up for us?" Since I am always fascinated with actual productive processes I happily agreed.

My first impression on approaching the plant was of masses of old-style seeders and plows parked on the nearby hillside. After passing the "maximum security" check at the gate, we entered to find all of the administrators together with many local political officials engaged in a meeting about the plan. They reluctantly detached the chief engineer to show us the plant and answer our questions. When I said that we had come to examine and photograph the new machines his face had a most distressed look. The yard of the factory was like a huge junk yard, with parts and materials dumped loose on the ground and exposed to the rain. We threaded our way out to a blacksmith shop in which some men were experimenting with an electronic device to tell if the potato planter were dropping the potatoes regularly. Obviously they were in the very first stage of development. Then we saw an unbelievably bad model of a rotary hoe. I asked: "Why do you start with this kind of a model when good models are already in use in many countries? Don't you know about them?" "Oh, yes. In fact we sent six engineers to the agricultural fair in Great Britain last year." "Did you buy any models?" "Yes." But he could show us only a six-year-old Polish model!

Finally he broke down and confessed that they had no new models that were ready for production. There was certainly no story about "new models" that the censor would think fit to print, and so instead I naïvely wrote a long letter of protest to President Novotný—not realizing that the irresponsible mismanagement of the plant was the result of the whole model of administration which Novotný himself headed.

At the Sixth Congress of Unified Agricultural Cooperatives, April 23–26, 1964, there was a display of latest Czechoslovak agricultural machinery. The sugar beet harvester was a beautiful thing, probably the best in the world for harvesting both the tops and beets. But nearby was a potato planter that had no provision for putting down fertilizer, and beet planters that had no provision for spreading in the row either fertilizer or herbicide. In my story of the Congress I pointed out that no one had noticed or protested these defects in the machines and that this indicated a lack of interest of farm leaders in farm technology. I also noted that the Congress had protested against the detailed and arbitrary control of the farms in the past—such as forbidding one of them to build a wash-up shower room for its barn workers even though the cooperative had the materials and men to build it themselves. President Novotný said: "Go ahead and build, and if someone takes you to court we will go in your place. . . . It is time to stop this useless tying down and stereotyped direction of agriculture. There is no need to tell when, what, and where to plant, cultivate, harvest, etc. These children's diseases of past years, I think, are behind us."

This was a revealing yet encouraging statement, but at the same time the Novotný administrative bureaucracy got the Congress to approve a directive that 54 percent of the land should be planted to grain in 1965 and 54.5 percent in 1966—and that was all that the bureaucracy needed to maintain the "petty tutelage" that the Congress had scolded them for. The censor refused to let my article about the Congress be printed, telling the editor: "If he had started out with a different standpoint he would have arrived at different conclusions."

The system of censorship hushed up complaints while the managers, engineers, and workers were lectured on their social duties. It should not be concluded that the people who resisted productive innovation were particularly selfish. In fact they may have been just as socially minded as those who lectured them—and who in turn resisted any changes in the economic-political model which was alienating the managers and workers from the progress in technology so essential to the success of socialism. Again we must insist that the scientific method is not to deny the facts as they are or to blame individuals, but to seek the sources of such attitudes of resistance to innovation—and to introduce effective remedies.

Among the proposed remedies are those which would economically (as well as morally) reward the innovators and those who accept innovation. This means such things as promptly adjusting prices of products and equipment to reflect socially necessary costs —a very difficult task which will require some combination of administrative and market pressures. If managers or workers refuse to introduce more productive methods they should be faced with a progressive decline in the relative price for their product, which would be reflected in their own incomes. This may mean a standstill in the wages of those working in older factories while the wages of those in more productive plants move upward. Obsolete plants should be renovated or closed. Such a policy implies also a greater differential in earned incomes than exists today in Czechoslovakia—perhaps almost as much as in the other socialist countries, but certainly not of the magnitude that characterizes the capitalist distribution of income where highest incomes come from ownership.

It will take some experimentation to find out how best to reward and stimulate change with economic incentives. Let no one think that it will be simply a matter of tinkering with the method of awarding bonuses, or the size of the social fund. A great variety of stimulators may be necessary to fit the conditions of different industries. Let us take another example to show that a broad frontal attack on the problem is needed in some cases. One of the sights that is most distressing to anyone concerned with efficiency or human dignity is to see women spreading manure in the fields by pitchfork. For a long time I thought that this was an example of male chauvinism in work assignment and of indifference to the mechanization of "women's work." Then on a cooperative farm I noticed a manure spreader standing idle while a tractor with a fork lift loaded the manure onto a trailer. From there it was dumped in piles in the field and women later spread it. When I asked why this labor-consuming method was used when they had the equipment for efficient operations the answer was: "The spreader does not work." "Why not?" "The axles burn off." "Why should they burn off if you grease them as you do those of the trailer?" No answer. Then, "As a matter of fact the women insist that we do it this way because otherwise there is no work for them this month and they need a minimum of work units [hours] to get paid."

Here, the bar to productivity was the fact that for the women any work was better than none. In the old days of individual farming they had taken up the slack winter months in all kinds of labor-consuming activity, including manure spreading, and quite a bit of folk art and other cottage industries. Such light industries were scorned by the central planners; no market or materials were provided and so the folk or cottage production withered away. This left the women even more dependent on make-work on the farms. In this case centralized planning, instead of eliminating make-work, has fostered it.

Now again there is some movement toward freeing the market for sales of handicraft products. But note that Prague as yet (1971) does not have a real "farmers market," although now it has some outlets for cooperatively produced pottery, embroidery, and other folk products. Properly organized, such cooperatives could, with very little investment, furnish much more attractive and productive work making hundreds of kinds of useful gadgets now missing from the socialist market. The mania for large-scale enterprises is subsiding in Czechoslovakia, and it is realized that a great deal of output could be obtained from small cooperatives that fitted their activities into the seasonal demands of agriculture, or perhaps even offered in the rural areas a steady alternative to unproductive work on the farm. Under the old system of centralized planning and management such small-scale operations were just a complication and headache for those compiling the plan. But, if partial decentralization is permitted, and it is recognized that it is not necessary to plan *all* the activities of *all* people, particularly of marginal workers, much additional and useful production could take place on a cooperative or even on an individual basis.

It is not just in agriculture that we find this make-work attitude and the accompanying resistance to mechanization and automation. Early in 1969 I visited a technical glass factory in rural Slovakia. It was a new plant, with some of the latest-type equipment in the world. But it had a curious and decisive contrast between fully automated work and other work being done by women sitting around in groups inspecting or packing the products of the automatic machines. The flow of materials and product that characterize a well-organized plant stopped abruptly shortly after the glass left the machines, and pre-industrial methods of handling began. This dichotomy of techniques was not accidental or the result of incompetent engineering, but arose from a conflict of purposes. One purpose was to provide employment in a rural area. The second was to produce technical glass products of high quality and cheaply. If inspection and packaging had been highly mechanized the plant would have failed in the first purpose. Here we have social and political policy in conflict with productivity. My own "feeling" is that the better policy, in view of the already very high level of employment, would be not to mix the technologies: to build the glass plant as a maximum-efficiency unit, and to provide low-investment cooperative or cottage work for the older women who might have difficulty in learning to supervise automatic equipment. In that way the costs of production could be more clearly known. As it is, part of the cost of production of the technical glass should be charged, not to the product, but to social welfare of the area. This is the kind of contradiction of aims that complicates much of the attempt to put socialist enterprises on a strictly cost-accounting basis.

Cost Accounting

One of the points about which Lenin was most insistent was that production should be on a strictly cost-accounting basis and that subsidies should be kept to a minimum. This has such a commonsense basis and is so fundamental to any orderly operation of an enterprise, to say nothing of the economy, that one might expect that this would be one of the most closely followed of Lenin's precepts. Actually it has been one of the most consistently violated. We have remarked before (p. 56) that in Czechoslovakia the centrally fixed prices gradually departed more and more from cost and market prices until a point was reached at which it was practically impossible to know which industries and enterprises were being subsidized and which were operating at a social profit. One industry might appear to be making a handsome profit, for example, but only because the prices set for its products were well above world prices. Another industry might be very efficient in terms of actual costs and quality, yet appear to be operating at a loss.

In the end there was almost endless bookkeeping and reporting, but very little knowledge of real costs, and even less use of the bookkeeping as a tool for understanding how to make the operations more efficient. Accounting became a means of inflating costs in order to obtain more subsidies, or to satisfy the requirements of the Plan or the higher bureaucracy. Its very form and lack of inclusion of *all* economic costs precluded its use as basis of planning and management. The bookkeeping went on, and economic decisions were often made without regard to whether the enterprise's books showed a profit or loss. This was the situation in other socialist countries as well as Czechoslovakia.

In the Soviet Union we find the First Deputy Minister of Agriculture, I. Volovchenko, a half century after Lenin wrote, reporting:

> The switch of state farms to operation entirely on a cost-accounting basis is a new important stage in their development. Appropriate economic and organizational measures, such as accurate planning, greater independence, an increase in procurement prices of some agricultural products, enhancement of the material incentives of production workers, have paved the way for successful implementation of this transition. Since July of this year (1967) 406 state farms (out of 12,189), including all state farms of the Estonian Republic and the Voronezh region, have been switched experimentally to a cost-accounting basis. The introduction of this efficient method of management will make it possible to enhance considerably the role of key economic factors on state farms, to make fuller use of available

reserves, to achieve stable profitability of each state farm. (*Selskaya Zhizn,* September 16, 1967.)

It must not be thought that the difficulty of using proper cost accounting was confined to agriculture. In the same year Y. Kvasha, in an article on concentration of production and small-scale industry, noted that "tens of thousands of units are without cost accounting." (*Voprosy Ekonomiki,* No. 5, 1967.)

Rather obviously some strong forces were operating to prevent the use of such an essential tool of good management.[17] We have already touched upon the main one of these. *The whole economy was being operated on essentially a "cost plus" basis.* As long as the central planners specified the volume of production required, and as long as that planned volume was the main goal of the enterprise, the central planners of necessity had to compensate the producing unit for its production. It was not realization of the investment by sales in the open market that counted, but producing at least the volume specified in the plan. And since, for accounting convenience, the plan targets came usually to be set in monetary terms, they were easier to fulfil if costs were higher. In this respect the plan targets had an effect very similar to the "cost-plus-percentage-fee" system of letting government contracts which became notorious in the United States and Great Britain during World War I for its encouragement of labor hoarding, waste of materials, and neglect of quality. The higher the cost the higher the profit. The centralized plan may have had elaborate subsidiary incentive payments for increases in productivity or savings in materials, but the fact remained that the main indicator was the volume of output and the surest way to attain that goal was to be wasteful in using

---

[17] Cost accounting is essential for good management, but it certainly does not insure good social management, or even efficient management of an enterprise. Robert McNamara, an expert in mathematical accounting and management, introduced the latest electronic computer techniques, and accounting devices such as PERT, into the Pentagon's procurement. Yet under his administration some of the most incredible wastes in world history took place, with not just millions but billions of dollars going into projects that had no value, even from the point of view of defending capitalist United States. For example, the "DEW line" (Distant Early Warning) radar stations were built in northern Canada and Alaska as a warning against bombers at a time when missiles were known to be the main danger. The B-52 bombers cost billions, yet are so vulnerable that until 1972 they were used in Vietnam only in the South where there was no anti-aircraft defense! "Make-work" for the United States capitalists is operating on a scale no other country can afford.

old methods to produce familiar products. It is in fact a tribute to the social consciousness of managers and engineers that the amount of waste induced by the quantity targets of the plan was not even greater.

Capitalism has as yet devised no sure remedy for the wastes of public contracting, but it has generally abandoned the "cost plus" method and substituted, wherever possible, competitive bidding, with special awards for savings in time and in costs. But this works only in the absence of monopoly or collusion. *If there is competition* and the "profit" of an enterprise depends upon its sales in the market, the managers have an immediate interest in proper cost accounting because only in that way can they know how to reduce unit costs and increase the margin between costs and gross income. We conclude that the central fixing of both targets for production and sales prices is the main reason that cost accounting has been so underdeveloped in the socialist countries.

But there are other important subsidiary reasons. One set of these reasons may be classed as political, the other as theoretical. On the theoretical side we may list the failure properly to understand what constitutes social costs. This shows up, for example, in the failure to count land as a cost. It was assumed that since land was socially owned there was no sense in making a charge for it since it would just be taking a sum out of one pocket to put it in another. This does not take into account the fact that there are many alternate and competing uses of land and that one test of whether a project is economically justified is the amount and kind of land it uses. The cost of any one project must include the "opportunity cost" of the next best use of the land. Reflections of this lack of accounting for land costs can be seen in the long periods in which busy streets are allowed to be closed, although this is partly due to failure to value properly the time and inconvenience of people. Costly land, and even buildings, are kept idle for years: for example, the closing of the many small shops in the historic part of Prague which could be highly attractive to tourists.

Similarly it was assumed that little or no interest should be charged on capital invested in public projects. Machinery was given to farmers and to factories, or loans made at a ridiculously low rate of interest which in no way reflected the true cost of the capital or the returns it could bring in alternative uses. The result was often that the care and full use of the equipment were neglected—and all means of calculating the true total cost of the commodity or service were rendered futile. Since the accounting did not serve that fundamental purpose, the managers and planners thought that they could be content with rudimentary accounting for that part of the costs with which the center happened to be concerned.

On the political side we should perhaps start with the near mania for secrecy—one of the basic devices by which any bureaucracy inflates its ego and protects itself from criticism. To this day some of the socialist countries refuse to publish such data as the differentials of income between the sexes and among different occupations. Costs of production, even of farm commodities, are kept secret, and this enables inefficient firms to avoid being shut down and protects from criticism autarchic and high-cost political projects such as the project of using domestic Czechoslovak iron ores. The secrecy also protected those who faked the accounts, and permitted some claims of successes which only years later were shown to be false.

Even the *methods* of accounting became a political football and, instead of judging the merits of an accounting system, labels such as "bourgeois" or "socialist" were attached. Czechoslovakia, as one of the most advanced industrial nations (and this was one reason for that high level), had well-developed systems of accounting under capitalism. The best known was that of Baťa, the shoe firm. One of its merits was that it showed the costs of different operations and functions, such as maintenance, and the total costs, including charges for capital and depreciation. Such advanced accounting methods were in widespread use in Czechoslovakia during the first postwar years and even in the first two years of the First Five-Year Plan.

As the Cold War developed and political trials got under way, one of the charges made against the accused economists and political figures was that they encouraged the use of accounting methods similar to those of Baťa—and this was argued as one of the reasons for disruption of production in some plants.[18] It was even charged

---

[18] Speech of Dr. Jaromír Dolanský, Minister-Chairman of the State Planning Board, to the Central Committee of the Czechoslovak Communist Party, "Work in a New Way—to Manage Our Economy in a New Way," *Plánované hospodářství*, September 1951, pp. 454–55.)

in the Slánský trial that the use of such "bourgeois accounting methods," instead of Soviet *"khozraschot"* accounting, was evidence of a plot to restore capitalism! (See Dr. Václav Kreysa, *Plánované hospodářství,* December 1952, pp. 820–21.) The result was that the Central Committee decided in July 1952 to go over to the "Soviet system of accounting" and ordered the Minister of Finance to put it into effect throughout Czechoslovakia by January 1, 1953.

Education

For two decades education in Czechoslovakia has played a dual role. The bureaucrats in power used education as a means of teaching dogma to the younger generation, of inducing conformity of response, and of producing technicians and scientists who, while expert in their own fields, did little thinking when it came to politics.

On the other hand parents, and many of the educators, wanted a broad education that went far beyond a technical knowledge, one that included languages and social sciences, history and literature. Even students who at the age of 14 (later 15) "went into industry" and as apprentices or learners were attached to a particular trade, spent half of their time in study, and those studies included both politics and languages. By comparison with some other countries, for example the United States, the amount of mathematical study required was also very high. In short, practically all children received at least the foundation elements of a scientific education. And there was no easy process of concentrating only on the most talented. It was assumed that *all* children (with the exception of a few mental cases) could be educated, and if the pupil lagged he received special attention. The regime was a demanding one for the teacher and students.

Within the school system itself there was an unceasing battle between the teachers and administrators who wanted an education that would develop a thinking social being and those who wanted only a high level of knowledge of what had been approved as history, a useful technical facility—but no originality. In the Cold War period of the 1950s there was no doubt that the dogmatists had the upper hand. Teaching was almost exclusively by rote, the textbooks arbitrarily selected what those in power felt it wise to let the pupils know. Whole episodes in history, even major events, were not mentioned, and such persons as Thomas G. Masaryk, the first President of Czechoslovakia, were either nonexistent or denigrated in a most outrageous manner. Any originality in the pupil was regarded as a dangerous symptom of anarchic spontaneity—a "bourgeois" characteristic. The theory was that the teacher was always right and that students should refrain from any show of spirit. At one time it was thought proper that children, even in the first grades, sit quietly in their seats with hands folded and not even whisper during "recess"! (Later the same principals of the schools encouraged the children to romp or play outdoors during recess for a total of at least one hour a day.)

One feature of this dogmatic approach to education deserves special attention since it was a source of much resentment and of unnecessary alienation from socialism. This was a discrimination against some children that arose from the theory that the leading role in a socialist society must be played by "the working class." Yet in practice it was found that in the competition for the right to go on to the free (with stipends) higher education it was the children of educated parents who had the advantage. Therefore quotas were set and children of those regarded as class enemies were denied the right to go to the universities. But in those years the Party bureaucracy was all too free in applying the label of "class enemy" and, as later admitted, thousands of cases of injustice resulted. The alleged "sins" of the fathers were visited upon the new generation that normally would have been quite loyal to socialism.

All too often the political test became the most important one—and this was true long after socialism had become internally secure. A close friend of mine had this experience: His daughter tried out for one of the few places available in a music conservatory. She passed the tests for her voice—but was failed in her interpretation of the history of the Communist Party. Another girl failed in the voice test, but passed the history test—and got the scholarship. The full irony of this was that a short time later the official version of that history was again changed—and so the music conservatory was left with a girl who could not sing and who had learned the wrong history. Much talent was lost in this way. It would have been enough to have required that all university students also learn to work with their hands—a much better guarantee that they would sympathize with the problems of workers than was the occupation of their parents.

There was a serious neglect of teaching the scientific spirit and methods during the 1950s and in many fields a disastrous decline of scientific experimentation. As one example we may take the school of agriculture at Tabor—one that in the First Republic had a fine reputation. The school had a farm with livestock and diversified crops. It had some modern machinery—but the students were not allowed to operate it. Instead they were required to learn obsolete methods, such as hand milking. The school had a botanical garden with some exotic plants, but it did not teach the pupils how to experiment with plant improvement.

In fact the students who did on occasion venture some interest in innovation were promptly squelched. As anyone who has done it knows, pulling flax by hand is back-breaking work. On one occasion, after a brigade of the students had been working at it for a couple of hours one of the students asked the teacher if this was not the kind of work that could be mechanized. The response of the teacher was to curse him roundly (in front of the girls) as a lazy bum. The teacher missed the chance of going over with the students the methods by which such a machine could be made (as it long ago had been). Instead he killed the initiative not only of that student but of others—and unwittingly exposed himself to them as an incompetent.

Teaching obsolete methods in a period of revolutionary technical development was the essence of the entire program of the school. Learning to recite textbooks by rote took all the joy and excitement out of agriculture, and turned what is preeminently a living and rewarding field of study into a very dull one. In fact, a very large part of the students dropped out or, if they finished the school, did not continue to work in agriculture. The bureaucrats bemoaned the loss of the costly social investment in education of these dropouts, but could not see that it was the dictatorial methods of teaching which had alienated the students.

One other policy added to this alienation, not just from agriculture but from what most of them assumed to be the methods of socialism. This was the assumption by the school administration that the students had no human or civil rights. The teachers assumed, for example, that they had the right to invade the rooms of the young women and men without even the courtesy of knocking! On the pretext of searching for young men, the male superintendent of the dormitories would burst into the rooms of the girls at bedtime. The young women regarded him as a Peeping Tom with power. This was how the bureaucracy used and corrupted the power assumed under the guise of the "dictatorship of the proletariat." Actually it had *nothing* to do with class warfare, and was not exercised by the "proletariat" but by petty people who by their arbitrary actions were undermining socialism.

When such students finally graduated and when some of them began to work on farms they encountered further bureaucracy which rendered largely useless their expensive education. One of my colleagues at the Academy, who had spent many years as the economist in a large cooperative, one day took me to see it. Over a beer I asked the young farm economist whether the cooperative earned a higher net return on potatoes or sugar beets. He had never figured it out! After a few minutes' calculation he and the co-op agronomist were surprised to find that it was potatoes. They were anxious to show us a new sugar-beet planter that could spread herbicide on the rows. But when we got to the field we found the new machine standing idle with a group of five men admiring it, while an old-style planter was busily planting seed without the herbicide. It did not matter, the co-op's agronomist explained: "The women need the work" of hoeing.

When we came to the potato planting we found the whole four-man crew in a frustrated and angry mood—they had planted only 2.5 hectares in a time they should have planted ten. The potatoes were too large and were jamming the planter. They were magnificent potatoes for the market, but had been neither sorted nor cut. The agronomist, even while looking at the load, at first insisted that they *had* been sorted: "Because I gave the order for them to be." At the age of 26 he was already the perfect bureaucrat! The system provided him with no real incentive to be a good manager. The old man on the loading wagon refused to cut the potatoes during his wait between planter trips. "Because it is women's work."

What is more, the potatoes were being planted without either herbicide or fertilizer: "This is good land and our plan is only 200 centnars (20 tons) per hectare. We will easily make that." In fact, as he gleefully reported later, the yield was 250 centnars. He had not thought that he could have fertilized and then fed the higher yield to the hogs.

In the cow barn the young veterinarian explained that he had only straw to feed his milk cows—and no urea and molasses to go with it. But, he added: "The reason the cows are lowing is that they are thirsty and we just do not have enough water here for them. If we dig more wells the people down the valley get less water from their wells." It would seem to be obvious that one can't produce milk without water, and without proper fodder. Yet the veterinarian in charge of the herd could not sell off his surplus cows since the quota of number of cows per hectare of land had been set from the center—a specific control that is a relic of the time when the peasants in Russia had slaughtered their cattle rather than give them into the collective farms. In defense of his professional understanding of the problem, the veterinary said: "I am already 37 cows below my quota—if the Party finds out I could sit [in jail] for a long time."

For me the most depressing part of the day was the almost complete lack of initiative of the three young men: the economist, the agronomist, and the veterinarian. Their costly education was not being used. The centralized system did not trust them to make even simple decisions about the farm's program and tried to get higher farm productivity by "petty tutelage"—a flood of directives and frequent inspections. So the young men waited for orders from above. They usually tried to carry them out even when they knew they were wrong—and they were doing no manual labor. The net result was that the farm, though considered to be a model, was producing at high cost and far below its potential. With proper incentives, good equipment, and adequate supplies of fertilizer and pesticides, and, above all, good management, the farm could easily have increased its output by 50 percent or more. But if it had produced more, under the old system it would not have been regarded as deserving continued economic rewards. Ways to pull its income down into line with less efficient cooperatives would have been used.

In spite of this typical reluctance to trust newly educated cadres, it is inevitable that their importance in society increase. Proper management of production becomes increasingly a matter of making the best possible use of scientific advances—and the scientists' judgment as to how to use science profitably must be relied upon more as that technology becomes less understandable to less educated managers. The educated technician is usually at least partly aware of his own importance and of the corresponding inability of laymen to understand some of the most vital problems of production. He therefore tends to resent dictation by those less educated, less informed persons.

This creates a sharpening point of trouble for the Communist Party since it continues to try to operate *in the era of socialism* under the slogan, correct in the 1917 revolutionary crises, that the "working class"[19] must play the "leading role." As a quickly rising proportion of the population becomes more highly educated and intellectual it becomes more difficult to pretend that the manual workers should continue to hold the key positions of power and decision-making. Yet for a long time the Party did push its old cadres into the top positions regardless of their educational qualifications. It is a temptation to give specific examples of such favoritism, but they would focus attention upon individuals, whereas the difficulty actually lies in the *concept* of management functions and of the "leading role" of the Party. In 1966, of 580 general managers in heavy industry in Czechoslovakia only 49 percent had a college education, and of 921 managers of chemical plants only 23 percent had higher education. A similar situation existed in other industries, with those holding managerial positions quite generally having less general or technical education than those forming their immediate staff. (Státní statistický úřad [State Statistical Office], *Zprávy a rozbory,* No. 5, 1967, p. 20.)

This pushing of "reliable" cadres who are not fully qualified for top administrative or technical work into leading positions has been a difficult problem from the early days of socialism. In speaking to the 11th Congress of the Communist Party of the Soviet Union on the problems of increasing the efficiency of production, Lenin said:

> The idea of building communist society exclusively with Communists is childish, absolutely childish. . . . The key feature is that we have not got the right people in the right place; that responsible Communists who acquitted themselves magnificently

---

[19] Usually not defined, but at the time it was originally formulated it meant primarily manual workers—certainly not university-educated scientists and technicians.

during the revolution have been given commercial and industry functions about which they know nothing.
(V. I. Lenin, *Selected Works,* English edition, Moscow, Vol. 3, pp. 694, 706.)

Curiously, some of the old Party cadres supported education, yet expected the younger generation to think exactly as they did. One worker that I know carefully fostered the education of his daughter as an economist. Then, when she became a good one, with ideas of her own about current problems, he shouted at her that she was only an intellectual and therefore her ideas could not be trusted!

Such distrust of intellectuals and specialists is directly contrary to Lenin's ideas:

Unless the Communist Party, the Soviet government and the trade unions guard as the apple of their eye every specialist who does his work conscientiously and knows and loves it—even though the ideas of communism are totally alien to him—it will be useless to expect any serious progress in building socialism.
(V. I. Lenin, *Selected Works,* Vol. 3, p. 660.)

CHAPTER 6

The System of Decision-Making and the Structure of Power

The concepts of how to manage the economy and the state used in the early models of socialism make it impossible to separate the role of one from the other. The management and decision-making were highly centralized and very often on a personal rather than organizational basis. It was assumed that those who held political power, as distinct from ownership power, would make the important economic decisions. All fundamental discussions of the efficiency of the system of economic management and decision-making also of necessity involve a consideration of the structure and use of the political power of the state. We begin the consideration of what appears to be an economic problem, such as the relationship of one price to another, or the incentives to increase productivity, and we find, time and again, that the root of the problem is political.

Management Responsibility

The first precept of sound management, whether of an enterprise or of the macro-economy, is that power and responsibility must correspond. Those who have the power to decide must also be responsible, and no one should be held responsible beyond his power of decision. It is usually assumed that confusions are reduced if the structure is as simple as possible and if the duties and rights of each office and executive are specified in relation to the other offices and executives in the organization. A written understanding of the hierarchy of powers and controls is almost always regarded as essential. This clearly understood structure of power must not be too rigid or it will tend to atrophy and retard technological and social change. But that is a distinct problem. At any one time the line of authority in an organization must be clear and it must be respected if efficiency is to be promoted and harmonious relations to prevail. If changed conditions require a new power structure, then that, too, must be agreed upon and clearly specified.

The power structure that developed in Czechoslovakia after 1948 was not as chaotic as that which prevails in some sectors of the capitalist structure. In the United States, for example, one of the difficulties in dealing with many social problems, such as water pollution or slum conditions, is that literally hundreds of local, state, regional, and federal agencies and organizations exist (in the Chicago area alone more than 1,200). Their authority is so ill defined and confused that action is often not possible. It is clear that each of these organizations was set up with some (usually good) purpose in mind, but their multiplication instead of facilitating action may, in the end, bring it to a halt. It is in the nature of these organizations of state power that once set up they tend to persist, often long after their original purpose has been fulfilled.[1]

In Czechoslovakia there was no such makeshift proliferation of units of state power, but the structure was complex enough, and a real ambiguity developed in powers and responsibilities throughout the economy. On the one hand were a group of bodies of state power concerned with the general formulation of policy, planning organizations, and those concerned with financial and other controls and information-gathering and processing. On the other hand stood the structure of the Communist Party, a structure which had evolved out of the Party's concept of its leading role.

Each of the Czechoslovak constitutions has provided that the supreme power and law-making authority of the state reside in the Parliament. The Parliament has established ministries dealing with the entire range of economic and social activities, and the ministers form a cabinet, usually referred to as "the government." There is a National Front, composed of representatives of the five political parties, which has as one purpose the harmonizing of policies for the development of socialism. The National Committees, with regional and local branches, act as the main regional and local gov-

---

[1] But note that in the *corporations* directly concerned with production, the structure of power and the mechanism of decision-making is simple, with a clear line of authority. There may be academic discussion as to whether ultimate power rests with the managers or owners, but there is no such doubt about the line of authority and responsibility in economic decision-making within the corporation.

ernment authorities. The Planning Office draws up the general plan of activity for the economy and (under the old system) set up the targets for production by enterprises in industry and state farms and cooperatives in agriculture. The State Bank works with the Planning Office in drawing up the financial side of the economic plan which is at the same time the budget for the state. It exercises independent supervision over financial matters, including the investments of the enterprises and agricultural organizations. The bank was primarily an instrument for controlling and enforcing the plan. It used administrative rather than economic powers to enforce the policies of the government and Party. The Trade Unions administer the Social Security system and have authority over many matters such as the safety and recreation of the workers. In the industrial enterprises and in the agricultural organizations themselves a separate line of authority exists.

In some enterprises the policy-making power is shared with a committee, whose members are elected by the workers. There is also a Central Committee for Statistics and Control with independent power to require reports on economic and other activities. All of these organizations have their powers and duties spelled out in legislation and by directives of the ministries and other authorities. The courts and police handle violations of the law and conflicts over the interpretation of the law. This was a legally constituted system complete in itself and with authority to deal with any problem of the economy or of society. It was a structure based on the elective power of the people and responsible to them.

But during the period from February 1948 until January 1968 practically all of the major decisions of policy were made outside of this structure by men at the top of the Communist Party. At the same time the structure of the Party assumed an expanding role in the administration of its policies, in directing the day-to-day work of the legally responsible agencies. As we have seen in Chapter 2, the authority of the Communist Party sprang from its revolutionary role, and rarely was spelled out in law. In practice this revolutionary power was strong enough to override the legal authority of the organizations and, over the years, these organizations became clearly subordinate to the Communist Party. They lost their initiative and tended to atrophy. For example, the Parliament no longer initiated important legislation, but "validated," usually by unanimous vote, the legislation already drawn up and submitted to it by the staff of the Central Committee of the Communist Party.

The Communist Party had its representatives in every organization and it always held the key post of personnel director. No one could hold a position of authority within an organization without the approval of the Party, and in some organizations appointments to *all* jobs had to be approved by the Party. This was not always any guarantee of loyalty to socialism since some people became experts in faking their records; and it was seldom a guarantee of competence since the records upon which the judgment was made stressed political factors, and frequently the decisive point was something quite safe for a bureaucrat, such as the occupation of the father.

All too often the decision *had* to be on this basis because the personnel director had no ability to judge the professional or other qualifications of the applicants. As a specific example, when I first came to the Economic Institute of the Academy of Sciences in 1954 the woman in charge of the personnel records, and de facto assistant on personnel policy, was a Mrs. P. She had little education and *no* training in economics and was completely unable to understand and pass judgment on the quality of any research work. At that time the man who was liaison representative of the Institute to the Party apparatus was a former ballet dancer turned journalist who also was not an economist. These two had power out of all proportion to their competence. The result was that the personnel of the Institute was of very uneven quality, and a good part of the work they turned out was not worth the paper it was written on. This situation was corrected only in 1962 when Professor Ota Šik was appointed Director of the Institute. Note that the reorganization of the Economic Institute was undertaken by the Party itself (and perhaps could have been undertaken only by it) when it was realized that the work of the Institute would have to be improved in order to help in the solution of Czechoslovakia's economic problems.

If the manager of any organization does not have the final word in the selection of his personnel he should not and ultimately *cannot* be held accountable for the performance of that organization, whether it be a research project or a factory unit. If the Communist Party insists on the priority of political tests that are independent of the particular work of the individual, then it should assume responsiblity for its judgments. But there is no practical way of requiring this. The Party as an independent and all-powerful organization cannot be called to account for its mistakes—except by itself. This does not mean that in some fields political reliability is not important. But where it is, for example in formulating political or economic policy, the test should be that of the policies being advocated or the work performed. That can best be judged by the specialists in the field, the responsible administrators and colleagues, many of whom are Communist Party members. Differences of opinion in regard to qualifications can be resolved in open discussion instead of by secret files which may contain false and irrelevant information.

Secret dossiers and police records are notoriously unreliable because informants know that they are generally not held accountable for the "information" they give. Yet this was just the kind of record upon which the Party placed its reliance. In the end such dossiers are more misleading than helpful—the only real test is the *work* of a man, and that can be judged only by his peers. As technology advances this difficulty of judging the competence of scientists and technicians becomes greater.

In the first period after nationalization it was sensible to have political control of the major enterprises, but as time passed the exercise of this political control came to be in sharp contradiction to the need for responsibility of management and also to the need for management that understood scientific technology. A very important part of the demand for decentralized management and more authority for the directors of enterprises was related to the idea that two decades after nationalization there was certainly no danger of the reversion of the enterprises to capitalism and that the primary need had become that of making the enterprises operate efficiently. To attain this end, the managers need the right to select their personnel and must be accountable for their work. In turn, a popular proposal, and one partly in effect, is that the enterprise itself (usually with some form of worker participation) should select its director or manager, subject in important cases to approval by the ministry. This establishes a clear line of responsibility under the new system. Where the enterprise has selected its manager, as at the Škoda works in Plzeň, persons of outstanding ability and political reliability have been chosen. This experience, however, is too limited to draw any firm conclusion other than that in the selection of personnel, as in other problems of management, power and responsibility must correspond.

It must not be concluded that the only form of intervention by the Czechoslovak Communist Party was in personnel matters. On the contrary, it concerned itself with all problems:

> Excessive economic centralism, though now being overcome, laid its imprint on party work. Party organizations dealt chiefly with production, the quantity and quality of goods produced by their factory, and the discussions were mainly over technical and economic problems. But not every party member, and certainly not every worker, could intelligently discuss the many details involved. The result was that executive personnel, who, of course, could competently examine such problems, acquired a dominant position on Party committees.
> (Miroslav Lab, *World Marxist Review*, December 1967, p. 42.)

Here we see that the Party, by substituting administration for a "leading role," became so involved in detailed production problems that it lost its leading role, and enterprise executives in some cases were actually leading the Party. There is no objection to having executives in a leading role, *except* that they could not be held accountable for the decisions made while wearing the Party hat. If the same decision had been made by the same people in their positions in the enterprise hierarchy the responsibility would have been clear. Nothing has been gained in having the duplicate consideration of production problems, and much has been lost in both valuable time and in accountability. And, if we allow ourselves to get ahead of the argument, the Party, when it began to give up this detailed work, as a part of the Czechoslovak understanding of the "new system of management," could pay much more attention to general *policy* problems. The net effect was that "The political work of Party members is acquiring more significance." *(Ibid.)*

In general social life it also became almost impossible to pinpoint the responsibility for certain irritating administrative rules and regulations, and the people—knowing that the Party made the most important decisions and took credit for all successes—naturally came to blame the Party for all failures. The ordinary bureaucrats, always anxious to extend their activities and powers, came to rule in an amazing number of spheres where there was no real justification for social controls. Encouraged by the predilection of the Party for control, the bureaucrats stuck their nose into many private affairs. A mother could not name her child as she wished unless by happy chance she wanted to give it only one name, and that name conformed to a "suggested" list.[2] I do not know the reason for this restriction (which incidentally causes endless confusion in the telephone directory). It seems to me that a mother could give a middle name to her child with no great harm to socialism. But the reason that you can name your pedigreed dog Maxim, but not Maximilian, is that Maximilian is too long to go in the space in the dog book! Such petty domineering may just seem ridiculous, but small and large irritations, repeated over and over, add up to a full-fledged annoyance and alienation.

Inspection, Controls, and Responsibility

The first question to be asked about any control is: "Is it worth its cost?" But as a rule this is the last question to be considered by a bureaucracy which tends to think that any activity which increases the payroll is a good one. We must think of "costs" not just in terms of money outlay, but also in terms of the results of the control in annoyance and loss of time of those being controlled. Controls can be of all kinds and all too many of them are unavoidable under modern conditions. For example, quality inspection of a part may be essential for the safety of aircraft. Other controls may be to insure honesty in financial matters or to protect social interests against individual greed. Systems of controls can be moral, and assume that the persons being controlled are honest. Or they can assume that all persons, including the inspectors, are dishonest. The latter is the ideal assumption for the proliferation of work of inspection and control. Credit for the duplications of the controls that grew up in Czechoslovakia must be given to the genius of the bureaucrats, rather than to Stalin, as some are wont to do. If everyone is assumed to be dishonest, then there must be not only a hierarchy of controls but competing systems of control. The theory of competing controls is that each group will do its job more thoroughly if it fears that some other person or agency will find an error or a fraud that it has overlooked.

---

[2] It cannot be assumed that this is simply an anti-Catholic device since most of the names on the list are those of Catholic saints.

One peak in this proliferation of control agencies was reached in Czechoslovakia in the 1950's. At that time, if a person had an electric accumulator heater installed, the head electrician on the job sat down and made out in handwriting a detailed itemization of every bit of wire, screws, brackets, etc. used. This control was intended to prevent loss of materials. In our case it was three pages long, and made out in *eleven* copies, the last six carbons of which were completely illegible. It was enough to know that the responsibility for control was dispersed among so many agencies to know that it could not be effective. In fact it was not. The installers refused to use and threw away good heavy copper wire, piping, and other materials which came with the heater when we bought it from a neighbor. Certainly in this case *all* of the controls were wasted—it would have been far better to have trusted the workmen in the first place to save all possible materials. This is seemingly a petty example, but if one multiplies the losses by thousands of cases daily throughout the economy, it becomes a problem of major significance. And then, if the cost of handling of all those illegible reports is added, and if we consider also the effect upon the dignity of workers being so minutely watched, we begin to realize the enormous social costs of this multiplication of control agencies.[3]

Everyone wants to think his work important and every agency seeks to prove by its results that it is indispensable. The way for an inspection team to show its worth is to find cases of error, and preferably of fraud. In our neighborhood in the early 1950s there was a small restaurant owned and operated by a man and his wife with no help. It was a quiet, clean place to go for simple family meals. The inspectors were annoyed to find Mr. Vitásek's books in perfect order. They required him to submit new reports, then more. The inspectors' zeal was intensified because the restaurant, being privately owned, was regarded as a blot on socialism, and so, as a

---

[3] One is tempted to quote Lenin again since his attitude toward such bureaucratic controllers is so refreshing: "Let us say frankly that the People's Commissariat of the Workers and Peasants Inspection does not at present enjoy the slightest prestige. Everybody knows that no other institutions are worse organized than those of our Workers and Peasants Inspection and that under present conditions nothing can be expected of this Commissariat. . . . I ask any of the present chiefs of the Workers and Peasants Inspection, or anyone associated with that body, whether they can honestly tell me the practical purpose of such a Commissariat. . . ." (Lenin, *Selected Works*, Vol. 3, pp. 776–77.)

part of the drive to liquidate "petty capitalist elements," they increased their harassment. They never found any errors in the books, but they did drive Mr. Vitásek out of business. Then they were satisfied, for almost immediately they caught the new manager of the restaurant cheating. Since then they have been able to send two managers to prison—clearly proving their vigilance. The restaurant meanwhile has become a low-grade beer joint—and Mr. Vitásek is a tramway conductor earning much more working far fewer hours.

Almost inevitably the inspection becomes a matter of checking upon compliance with routine (and often unimportant matters) as well as on the flow of funds. The inspectors increase their importance by requiring more reports and in more detail—and may miss entirely or not understand the significance of non-routine developments. And not understanding, they not infrequently use their power in a bureaucratic manner to kill initiative. The Plan for 1968 for Rožmberk Castle in South Bohemia called for earnings from tours of 40,000 crowns and a subsidy of 80,000 crowns. This was in line with experience of the previous two decades at the castle. But the new caretaker started up night tours, complete with ghosts, and converted one of the dungeons into a wine cellar. The result was an income of 180,000 crowns, no need for any subsidy, and repayment of costs of all improvements in one season. One might think that this would please the inspectors and that the caretaker would at least get some moral if not material encouragement. Instead, the inspectors were furious at the failure to fill out some reports in time (he had pleaded for a part-time bookkeeper) and even counted match boxes, post cards, and empty beer bottles in the vain hope of finding some error. It did not matter at all to them that the new caretaker had recognized and saved from further deterioration valuable paintings that had long been neglected. In the end they offered an insulting 300 crowns as a "bonus" for the entire staff for the season. Not just incidentally, from January to August 21, 1968, the inspectors were quite friendly. After that they again relapsed into pin-pricking bureaucratic methods.

Censorship

Such methods were just a part of the all-embracing system of controls and petty tutelage that characterized the policy of overcentralized decision-making. Under it, it was expected that all good ideas and all sound policies would come from the top hierarchy. Any idea that did not originate there was suspect. From this concept came the idea that controls were for the purpose of obtaining strict conformity with the ideas and programs of the men at the top and, as a part of this, the protection of the leadership from criticism. The next move was to take preventive measures so that the minds of citizens should not be contaminated with unapproved thoughts. An elaborate system of censorship developed which became the screen through which all ideas had to pass. The censors, of course, *could not* be experts in all of the scientific and cultural fields in which they made judgments. Yet they did not hesitate to confiscate scientific and other books coming from abroad for libraries and individuals, even those intended for the Academy of Sciences. At one time (and again now) this was a serious handicap to scientific work. The censors had the power to cut off not only information but even the suggestion that experimentation might be useful in some fields.

Some years ago I wrote a short article for *Zemědělské noviny* (Agricultural News) in which I noted that the U.S. Department of Agriculture had warned that the sex hormone, stilbestrol, could be dangerous if used on broiler chickens which might be eaten by children or pregnant women. My article simply suggested that tests be made before this hormone was used on the chickens. But the censor refused to permit the article to appear, "Because stilbestrol is already being used here." Here censorship, which nominally had the purpose of protecting socialism, is turned into the protection of a policy decision which may or may not have been correct. The experimentation and discussion which would be necessary for a scientific decision was arbitrarily cut off.

Any censorship is in sharp contradiction to the scientific method which requires full information. As science becomes more important in the working of the economy the conflict between censorship and science becomes so significant that it must be resolved. There is only one solution which is tolerable and that is the curtailment of censorship—and finally its practical abolition. This is true, of course, not only for economic and scientific reasons but because censorship is a primary limitation of democracy. Without the freedom of information, of the press, radio, and television, there can be no effective political democracy. And if political democracy is denied over a long period, even if this denial is made in the name of the class struggle, the quality of economic democracy tends to decline, and art and culture to stagnate. Before 1957 the Czechoslovak film directors were subject to strict censorship, and their films tended to be mediocre. After that censorship was very much eased and within a few years the films from this country developed a worldwide reputation for inventiveness and quality and incidentally, some films such as "The Shop on Main Street," also contributed to ethical understanding.

With censorship the governing group can protect itself from open criticism, but censors are never content with just that. Gradually they extend the scope of their arbitrary judgments, until the semblance of monolithic unity of thought and culture is attained. At this point the newspapers become almost unreadable, about the only thing that is read by many persons is the sports page where competition and excitement still prevail. The dullness itself becomes a factor alienating people, particularly young people, from the controlled society.

Starting with the intent to protect a particular form of society, censorship leads to the deadening of all discussion and the limitation of essential originality. Along with this go the pretensions of the bureaucracy to infallibility, which further alienates educated minds. In the end censorship builds up antagonisms to itself and serves mainly to keep the bureaucracy from knowing how unpopular it has become. This is one of the gravest dangers to socialism and especially to the Communist Party, which has no effective way of knowing which of its actions are popular and which are resented. Of course there are many indicators of the main trends in thinking.

One of these, known by Party officials, but only by observation by the public, was the drastic decline in the number of young people attracted to the Party in the later years of the Novotný era. By January 1, 1968 only 15.3 percent of all Communist Party members in Czechoslovakia were under *30* years of age and of those under 30 only 9 percent were in factory or other local policy-making bodies of the Party. In the entire network of Party regional committees only one person was under 25 years of age! (*Czechoslovak Life,* January 1969, p. 16.) Even the leaders of the official youth organization were beginning to get gray. The fact that this decline occurred despite the advantage that Party membership gave to certain careers, finally alarmed all but the most complacent of the bureaucrats. It became necessary for the Party itself to examine the causes of this alienation of youth, and particularly of the educated youth.

Dictatorship and Alienation

We have found that the major cause of dissatisfaction with the centralized system of economic management was that, after considerable initial success, it began to operate less efficiently than a socialist model could and must operate. Apart from this, yet inseparably linked to it, was the dictatorial use and abuse of political power. All attempts to change the economic model to make socialism work more effectively encountered the fact that the top control group in the Party could and did use completely arbitrary methods to prevent changes of the economic and political model. Even discussion *within* the Party was limited. For example, Professor Ota Šik, even though a member of the Central Committee of the Communist Party, was forbidden for a five-year period to address Party meetings. Other Party members, such as Zdeněk Hejzlar, who had dissented from some policy of the control group, were not even permitted to live in Prague. And if one had the temerity to suggest that the methods of the Party itself or its structure could be improved upon, as Čestmír Císař did when he was head of the Cultural and Ideological Bureau of the Central Committee, he might find himself exiled to work on some mission or embassy outside of Czechoslovakia.

This was relatively mild treatment compared with that handed out during the earlier period of the dictatorship of the Party in the 1950s, but it was sufficient, with those earlier repressions still fresh in mind, to induce conformity in most people. But the conformity was matched by resentment at these repressive measures, and a fundamental doubt that such measures were any longer necessary in Czechoslovakia.

That fundamental doubt about the need for the dictatorial measures arises from the fact that *before the major represessions began, socialist power had been consolidated in Czechoslovakia.* By the end of 1948 the capitalist class had no significant economic base of power. Only a small part of production and trade remained in private hands. In agriculture most of the large estates had been taken over. The power of the small capitalists and middle farmers to exploit their laborers had vanished, since the socialized sector of industry offered employment to anyone who thought that he was being paid unfairly by the private sector. The greatest repressions of the small private enterprisers and individual craftsmen did not take place until 1950 and 1951 and by that time the socialized sector of the economy had demonstrated such success that all real danger of counterrevolution was past. Ironically, as we have noted, this success that made the illegal and dictatorial methods unnecessary, also was a factor reducing the protest against them.

In any event, exercise of dictatorial power on behalf of the workers against the class enemy is one thing. Illegal use of police power against those who are not class enemies is quite another. *None of the trials was against capitalist groups.* Instead, in the weeks from January to March 1951 a total of 480 *public* trials took place. Of those tried in Bohemia 39 percent were workers! (K. Kaplan, *Nová mysl*, No. 7, 1968, p. 910.) Thousands of individual craftsmen, who up to that time had been friendly to socialism, and who had nothing to gain from a return to capitalism, were driven from their work and embittered. They were unorganized and were never shown to have made any plans, let alone to have participated in any *action*, against socialism. The experience in other countries, as well as here, indicates that the action taken against these small producers weakened, rather than strengthened, socialism.

As early as 1954 it was recognized in Hungary, for example, that the repression of small producers had deprived the people of essential services and was also seriously restricting the supply of some kinds of apprentices. By that time there were only 15 apprentices in the small-producer's sector in the entire country! After 1956 small producers were allowed to employ three skilled workers and three apprentices. By 1969 there were some 76,000 such producers, who employed 16,000 skilled workers and 15,700 apprentices. Regulations are simple and nonbureaucratic. If such a producer employs only one worker and one apprentice and earns less than 4,000 forints a month, he pays a fixed tax and need make no other report. These small private producers in Hungary not only perform valuable services for the home market, they also produce substantial amounts for export. (*Rudé právo*, March 6, 1969.)

In Poland the situation is quite different, with most of agriculture on a private basis and a whole network of private enterprises. In 1968, there were some 9,000 private industrial enterprises, about 33,000 private restaurants, 15,000 private shops, and 160,000 independent craftsmen in the cities. Together they produced products and services valued at 3,000 million zlotys, or about 20 percent of the national income. The monthly income of many of these private owners ranges up to 10 and 20 thousand zlotys, far above those of an average workman. (*Rudé právo,* December 9, 1968.)

Such a degree of private enterprise may, or may not, seriously weaken socialism—that is for the Poles to decide. Here, when there was talk of restoring some small craftsmen or producer cooperatives, no such extensive private enterprise was thought of. Instead, some system closer to the Hungarian model was contemplated, and (up to the invasion) no legislation had even been drafted. The only forms of private enterprise were the few private cab drivers and some farms in isolated areas where it was not convenient to form cooperatives. We repeat, these remnants of capitalism were no threat to socialism in Czechoslovakia.

The Trials and Rehabilitation

We do not propose to review the political trials,[4] but rather to point to their political significance and to the reason why the demand for corrective action has been so persistent. In the first place, the Communist Party has accepted full responsibility since it ordered the trials to take place. At the same time it is a matter of history that agents of Beria, then political head of state security police in the Soviet Union, were the initiators and supervisors of the *major* trials. Agents Makarov and Likhachev arrived in 1949 and began an active hunt for Trotskyite conspirators. These men worked with the Czechoslovak security police and relied mainly

---

[4] A fine series of three articles on the trials was published by K. Kaplan in *Nová mysl* (Prague), Nos. 6, 7, and 8, 1968. Kaplan worked for many years in the Institute for History of the Communist Party and as a member of the Central Control Commission of the Communist Party. By 1969 he came under severe attack for his revelations about the trials. Many books in English now discuss the trials, for example, Artur London, *The Confession,* Morrow, 1970; Eugen Loebl, *Sentenced and Tried,* Elek, London, 1969; Josefa Slanská, *Report on My Husband,* Hutchinson, London, 1969.

upon the method of "confessions." They sent their reports to Beria who was the Party man in charge of security. Beria reported to Stalin and Stalin sent the "evidence" to Gottwald. Just how much independence the Czechoslovak Party had at that point is a moot question. The fact is that the Central Committee directed State Prosecutor Jiří Urválek to begin the trials and handed him a sheaf of confessions upon which to proceed. Beria agents Bojarski and Likhachev also managed the Slánský trial. Their moment of glory did not last much beyond the time of their victims since they were executed along with Beria after Stalin died.

The main victims of the trials were members of the Communist Party itself; a large number of them were from the top leadership, and a highly disproportionate number of the victims were Jews. The charges were high treason, conspiracy against the state, espionage, and various forms of sabotage. The evidence was manufactured and confessions obtained by keeping the prisoners isolated from each other, by use of torture and other refinements such as mental fatigue, a low-calorie diet, solitary confinement, and confrontation by "confessions" of others. Only a few were able to hold out against these methods. The public generally knew nothing about these methods until long after the trials and assumed that the "confessions" gave a correct picture of conspiracy and crimes. Censorship carefully hid even the number of trials and executions. It was not until March 21, 1969 that *Rudé právo* published the fact that between 1948 and 1952 a total of 178 persons had been executed for alleged political crimes!

Since the people did not know that the evidence in the trials were faked, and since they seemed to be protecting socialism, there was even, for a time, wide support for the trials. There was among the workers and Party members unquestioning faith in the integrity of the Party. Paradoxically, this faith was one of the most effective weapons used by the police investigators in obtaining confessions from the victims. The victims also believed that the trials *must* be serving some social purpose.

It is now obvious that at least in some cases there was no such purpose. Let us take only one case from among the more than 70,000 victims of such trials. V. L. was arrested while acting as assistant to Josef Pavel, then Deputy Minister of Interior. V. L. was charged with "personnel sabotage." He was kept three years in solitary confinement, during seven months of which he was on a diet of about 1,500 calories per day. His weight dropped to only 116 lbs. (at 5'8" height) and interrogations lasted all night, once for seven days in a row. Finally he promised to write a "criticism of the Ministry." And while he took a month to do it he ate and rested. When the police investigators finally deciphered his manuscript and found no evidence for prosecution they were furious. With no evidence at all they "persuaded" the judge at a secret trial to give V. L. 16 years in prison. No appeal was possible.

V. L. had not even selected those men whose appointment the investigators regarded as proving "sabotage." The final irony came after he had served five years in prison and, on being released, found that *not one of the "unreliable" persons he was sent to prison for allegedly hiring had been prosecuted.* Some of them had been promoted to important posts!

Czechoslovakia is a small country, and when you have more than 70,000 such cases the injury is pervasive. And when the truth finally became known the resentment was also general. Add to this the injustices done to tens of thousands of small farmers and artisans whose small shops and farms were confiscated. And other thousands who lost jobs because they had a brother in Brazil, or because they had fought in the International Brigade in Spain, or had been a member of the Sokol sports organization. Altogether the bill of indictment against the organization responsible for this illegality became too large to be ignored. The people wanted a full and public "rehabilitation" of those to whom grave injustice had been done. They also demanded that those directly responsible for the injustices be removed from positions of power. Of course some, such as Václav Kopecký, had died, and others, such as Vilém Široký and Alexej Čepička, had long since been removed from office.

But the First Secretary of the Communist Party and President of the Republic, Antonín Novotný, had been one of the inner circle of the Party most responsible for the trials and *the* person most responsible for delaying rehabilitation after 1956. Until January 1968 he headed the group that obstructed a thorough reexamination of those trials. He at the same time led the conservative opposition to proposals for reform of the economic system. The Czechoslovak people had long been ready and eager to move ahead to a higher, more democratic stage of socialism. Novotný and his group barred the way. His removal from power became a test of the ability of the Communist Party to lead the people in this advance.

Below Novotný were hundreds of lesser officials and bureaucrats, at all levels of the Party apparatus and of the government, who had abused their powers and actively assisted in the illegal acts. The people, and a growing number of Party members, became more and more insistent that the time had come for the Party "to clean its shield" and in doing so to remove from power all those who had committed crimes or benefited from them. Even more fundamental than this was the demand for a change in the dictatorial, irresponsible, and unconstitutional system of power that had made possible these colossal blunders which had inflicted such unnecessary hardship and loss of life. The Party officials at all levels ignored the legally constituted and responsible governmental bodies, often making individual decisions without even Party directives and in disregard of the relevant laws.

We do not think that it would be correct to conclude that Novotný and his group were extraordinarily incompetent or vicious. Quite the contrary, they acted as one would expect of men exercising irresponsible power over a long period of time. They became guilty of illegal acts because they extended the powers of the dictatorship of the proletariat into the period in which the power of the capitalist class had been broken. They used the powers of dictation after—long after—the class struggle had been won. They exercised these powers, or allowed the police to exercise them on their behalf, not to protect socialism but to preserve an obsolete, overcentralized model of it. Their arbitrary use of power became not a "dictatorship of the proletariat" or even a "dictatorship of the Party," but simply dictatorship.

No one should be surprised at this result or say that they had not been warned in time. In January 1926 (a decade before he began his own bloody purges) Stalin wrote: "The Party exercises the dictatorship of the proletariat." But then he continued:

> Hence to talk about the dictatorship of the Party *in relation to the proletarian class,* and to identify it with the dictatorship of the proletariat, is tantamount to saying that in relation to its own class the Party must be not only a guide, not only a leader and teacher, but also a sort of state power employing force against it. Therefore, whoever identifies dictatorship of the Party with the

dictatorship of the proletariat tacitly proceeds from the assumption that the prestige of the Party can be built up on force, which is absurd and absolutely incompatible with Leninism.
(J. V. Stalin, *Problems of Leninism,* Moscow, 1947, pp. 140 and 144. Stalin's emphasis.)

CHAPTER 7

The "New System"

Clearing the Road for Advance

After the death of Stalin in 1953 and, even more, after Khrushchev's partial exposure in 1956 of the crimes of the Stalin regime, the Novotný administration became an obsolete anachronism. It took twelve years, however, before Novotný was deposed, and we should ask why it took so long. First, when a regime controls all of the means of power, the jobs, the police, the army, the press and radio, it is not a simple matter to expose and discredit it. It must first have visible failure, such as the failure of the economic plan from 1962 to 1963. Such a failure opens the eyes of ordinary people to other shortcomings, particularly to the lack of freedom to criticize and the indifference of the bureaucracy to the problems, their lack of a program for improvement.

The awakening in Czechoslovakia came gradually and in many sectors of the society. We have already noted that as early as 1957 the film industry, using the lever of unprofitability of the dull films that resulted from dogmatic restrictions, had attained a large measure of freedom. The film directors had promptly demonstrated the higher cultural level that the new freedoms encouraged. There was deepening unrest and sharper and more profound criticisms in education and among the writers. A new high point of protest came in June 1967 at the conference in Prague of the Writers' Union, which at that time was in the lead in opposing Novotný. At that conference many Czech writers, among them Antonin J. Liehm,[1] spoke out against the ill-informed petty tutelage of the party's cultural dictators.

Liehm told the conference:

. . . whenever people are deprived of political rights, whenever

---

[1] Antonin J. Liehm was born in Prague in 1924. From 1960 to 1967 he was one of the editors of *Literarni noviny*. After his speech at the Writers' Union conference he was, along with Klima and Vaculík, expelled from the Communist Party. He is now in exile, teaching art and film criticism in New York.

a society lacks a functioning political system commensurate with its level of development, culture continues to perform political tasks until normal political processes are restored. . . .
In my opinion, the cultural policy of a socialist state has a twofold task: To liberate culture from the dictates of power, and to liberate culture from the dictates of the market.
(*The Politics of Culture,* translated and published by Grove Press, N.Y., 1972, pp. 42 and 66.)

It can be understood that such a concept of culture liberated from both Party dictatorship and that of the market would infuriate people who still clung to the concepts of control of culture imposed by Andrei Zhdanov under Stalin. Nominally those concepts centered on the idea that socialist culture should serve the people—an idea that it is not easy to quarrel with. In practice the top people in the Party, who too often had little cultural understanding themselves, decided that what they did not like was bad for socialism. Culture was put in a straightjacket and told to flourish.

The long cultivation of the minds of students and the general Czechoslovak population by novelists, writers, and teachers was essential preparation for the fact that the deep unrest over the economic shortcomings and political repressions took the form of a rational program of advance instead of wildly violent protest. When the opportunity for action came the people knew what they wanted: a new form of socialism, not a retreat to obsolete forms of society. They wanted a return to the rule of law, to the functioning of the elected agencies of government and a curbing of arbitrary powers. They wanted the administration of justice to be returned to the Ministry of Justice, the powers of the prosecutor to the prosecutor, the powers of the courts to the courts.

One of the teachers and critics most influential, particularly in forming the opinions of students, was philosopher and professor at Charles University, Eduard Goldstücker.[2] Goldstücker was one of

---

[2] Eduard Goldstücker, born in Slovakia in 1913; Ph.D. Charles University, Prague 1939. Emigrated to England 1939 and active in Czech Government in Exile; Deputy Ambassador in London 1947–49; Envoy to Tel-Aviv 1950–51; imprisoned 1951–55; 1956–69 professor and later Pro-Rector of Charles University. Member of Parliament and head of the militant and very influential Union of Czechoslovak Writers, 1968–69. After the invasion an exile in England and America; Professor University of Sussex.

those who set the high moral tone of the demands for change, one who put in philosophical, yet specific, terms the aspirations of the ordinary people and students. He said:

> In Czechoslovakia we have every necessary condition for the introduction of the democratic element into our socialist structure. We had all the conditions we needed to make the transition from the dictatorial phase of our socialist revolution to the phase where we could achieve the original aims of the revolution, namely, the liberation of man from as many oppressive factors as possible. The transition of the revolution from the dictatorial to the democratic phase is a very difficult problem. It is the most difficult of revolutionary problems. No revolution has yet succeeded in making that transition. We in Czechoslovakia have a very concrete hope that we can succeed. . . . Human problems still existed, but in 1968, as soon as the first ray of hope reached our people that socialism and freedom could be combined, we witnessed in Czechoslovakia an incredible flowering of the new qualities in people throughout the country.
> (*The Center Magazine,* November/December 1970, p. 65.)

It was this high cultural and moral tone which formed the character of the political, economic, and social demands which the people of Czechoslovakia made upon the Communist Party and government. This is why the "new system" of planning and management as expressed in the "Action Program" is such a unique and vital document. I venture to predict that in years to come it will be regarded as a bench mark in human progress. Let us examine closely these critical developments.

The new system of planning and management in Czechoslovakia had its origins in objective economic and social developments outside of the Communist Party. But the actual reform could come only from within the Party itself. The pressures for change were a long time in maturing. At the time of the 12th Congress of the Communist Party in Czechoslovakia in December 1962, the economy was in serious difficulty and there was much dissatisfaction over the political trials and the reluctant and partial admissions of judicial error. There was a strong rank-and-file demand for more information, for more democracy generally and in the Party itself. The protest against bureaucracy was particularly sharp, and in his report First Secretary Novotný said:

The "New System"

Comrades! One of the basic tasks in building and developing of socialism is the more and more broad and consistent practical realization that the people, who are the creators and owners of all values of society, administer and manage this state.
(*XII sjezd Komunistické strany Československa* [Report of the 12th Congress of the Communist Party of Czechoslovakia], Prague, 1962, p. 46.)

It was typical of the old leadership that they could in one speech assert that the "people" ran the state, soundly denounce "petty bureaucratic tutelage," and yet announce new ways of dictation:

The Agricultural Commission of the Party Central Committee will become the center for the *daily* management of agriculture. (*Ibid.*, pp. 28 and 33. My emphasis. G.W.)

This was a failure to understand either the mood of the progressive members of the Congress or the fundamentals of agricultural management. The Central Committee *could not* be a center for *daily* management of agriculture, a function which must be decentralized if it is to be efficient, if it is to be able to respond in time to such elementary factors as changes in the weather. But the *attempt* at such supervision, not only in agriculture but throughout the economy, increased the irritation of the people, including Party members, with the Novotný group.

By the time of the 13th Party Congress in mid-1966 the economic problems had become more complex and difficult and the demands for both political and economic action more insistent. The Congress adopted a series of resolutions, one of which stated that it was necessary:

To complete, and *introduce*, from next year on, *the improved system of planned management throughout the economy.*
(Emphasis in original. *Report of the 13th Congress*, pp. 389–90.)

This emphasis indicated impatience with the slowness of the Novotný administration to respond to the increasingly acute economic and management problems and with its heel-dragging attempts to avoid carrying out the resolutions of the 12th Congress.

On the political side, the resolutions of the 13th Congress were even more significant. They indicated that the members of the

Party understood the root cause of the delays in making economic changes and wanted to move ahead to a more democratic form of socialism. The resolution read in part:

> The dictatorship of the proletariat has fulfilled its main historic mission in our country. . . . The development of our society is closely connected with an extension of socialist democracy, with the active participation of the working people in administration and management. . . . The development of democracy must go hand in hand with strengthening of a scientific and professional approach to social management.
>
> The basic pillar in the system of organs of state power and administration, and the basic link in developing the system of socialist democracy, are the (elected) National Committees.[3] We shall gradually extend their social, economic and educational activity so that they may develop into organs of real self-administration by the people.
>
> (*Ibid.*, pp. 31 and 404.)

These documents of the Communist Party expressed a new policy, one that recognized that it was not possible to continue with the dictatorial methods of the past and at the same time have effective democratic administration. What is not explicitly stated, but was known to all, was that it was those dictatorial methods which led to the atrophy of the local and regional National Committees —the duly elected bodies for "social, economic and educational activity" and administration. It was less difficult for the progressive members of the Party to gain approval for such a statement of policy because nominally democracy had been the goal of socialism from the very beginning. It was far harder to force through the radical changes needed in administrative *practice*. Here resistance was met not only from the Novotný group itself, but from a large section of the Party bureaucracy which had a vested interest in "business as usual."

After the 13th Congress the tension increased between those members of the Party, including members of the Central Committee, who wished to carry out the resolutions and those who feared genuine democracy. The "old guard" which wished to preserve the *status quo* still had much power and held the key positions. It

---

[3] Local government and administrative bodies.

could, and did, use that power quite freely, shifting out of important positions those who wanted change, ordering others to keep silent. The essential weakness of the "old guard" was that it had no program for solving specific problems. And the problems called aloud for solution. Jiří Hendrych, representing Novotný and the Presidium of the Central Committee, could lecture the Writers' Congress in June 1967 upon the need for Party discipline, they could expel some members from the Party and take over the writers' journal in September. The Presidium arbitrarily took over the building and presses of the Writers' Union and put out its own "literary" journal—but it could not get competent writers to write for it, nor people to read it. Readers expressed support for the moral position of the writers by refusing to buy the substitute paper. The Novotný group still held the power—but it had lost the people.

In October 1967 the police made the mistake of breaking up a candlelight protest parade of students who had been driven to spontaneous action by the repeated shutdown of electric lights in their dormitories just at examination time, by poor food and other grievances. They chanted, "We want light." The parade was unorganized and there were not even cameras there to record the event. About six students were injured—altogether not enough to rate a headline in many cities of the world. But the Czechoslovak people were indignant: "Who do the police think they are? Beating up our students!" A short film of stills of bandaged heads, of doctors describing the injuries and of professors of law saying that the police had acted in violation of the Constitution, was shown to angry audiences all around the Republic. The harsh police action was taken as a symbol of the indifference of the Novotný administration to peoples' problems—problems which in some cases could be easily solved. In this case nearly all the student demands were met within a week after their demonstration—but the fat was in the fire as far as the students were concerned. They had learned the value of active political participation, and added their voice to those of factory workers who, with increasing vehemence, were demanding that Novotný and his government resign.

One of the most effective arguments against Novotný was that he held too much power and, that instead of using it to carry out the resolutions of the 13th Party Congress, had used it to block their realization. This was particularly important to the thinking of older members of the Central Committee: Novotný was preaching "party discipline" but sabotaging the decisions of the supreme body of the Party. By the time of the December 1967 meeting of the Central Committee Novotný had lost control of the majority, and it was decided in principle to separate the functions of First Secretary from those of the Presidency. It was a tense time, with a mysterious order mobilizing part of the army. Novotný denied any knowledge of the mobilization. The Minister of Defense, Bohumír Lomský, told an unbelieving television audience that no such alert had taken place. The tension, and the fear of a military coup, was eased on January 6, 1968, when the Central Committee announced that Novotný had resigned as First Secretary and had been replaced by Alexander Dubček.[4] The first phase of the political crisis was over.

However, Novotný was still President and as such Commander in Chief of the Army. There remained widespread fears that in some way his group would use these powers to block further changes. One of the first acts of the new Dubček leadership was to relax in practice censorship of the press, radio, and television. For the first time in many years the people had an effective means of calling attention to illegal or antisocial acts of public officials. One of the first to be exposed was Major General Jan Šejna, a protégé of Novotný and his political representative in the army. Šejna was charged with selling to cooperatives in military areas seed that he was supposed to have distributed free. His "take" was rumored to be several hundred thousand crowns. On February 25 Šejna fled to the West. He went on a diplomatic passport and in one of the two foreign-made cars owned by Novotný's son. Novotný widened the credibility gap by trying to pretend that he hardly knew Šejna. This shattered his remaining authority. He could no longer resist the demand that he also give up the Presidency. On March 22 he

---

[4] Alexander Dubček, First Secretary of the Central Committee of the Communist Party from January 1968, to April 1969 was born in Slovakia in 1921. His father was one of the skilled workers who volunteered to help in the Soviet Union in its first years. Young Alexander received his early education there and, after fighting in World War II with the forces liberating Czechoslovakia, he worked in a factory in Slovakia. He then returned to the Soviet Union, completing his studies and was graduated *cum laude*. Upon his return he became a Communist Party functionary in Slovakia. Part of his immense popularity lay in his open honesty and in the fact that he was *not* a slick politican. He now is an ordinary worker in Slovakia.

resigned and on March 30 the Parliament elected General Ludvík Svoboda[5] as President. In keeping with the new democratic spirit, for the first time in Czechoslovak history the President was elected, not by a show of hands, but by secret ballot. The old cabinet resigned, and President Svoboda commissioned Oldřich Černík[6] to form a new one which was sworn in on April 9.

The way finally appeared to be cleared for a rapid advance to a much more democratic and attractive form of socialism. A euphoria prevailed that had not been known in Czechoslovakia for nearly a generation. Confidence was growing in the Party, many young people were joining. A complete change in attitude of people toward their government took place. The political indifference and feeling that it was not possible for ordinary people to have any voice in political affairs was replaced by a rejuvenation of many long inactive organizations, the trade unions, the women's and youth organizations, and the elected governmental bodies and Parliament itself. Local Party meetings under Novotný's tutelage had been routine and incredibly boring, with some locals holding only nominal meetings.[7] After January it was not uncommon for meetings to last from the close of work at 2:30 until nearly midnight—and then the routine was to rush home and turn on the radio or

---

[5] President General Ludvík Svoboda, a farmer's son born in 1895, deserted the Austro-Hungarian army and crossed over to fight with the Russians during World War I. Later he taught in a military academy in Moravia, and when the Nazis occupied Czechoslovakia his whole family joined the resistance. He helped to organize and commanded the Czechoslovak army that fought alongside the Soviet troops in the liberation of Slovakia. He was decorated many times by the Soviet Union. In 1945 he signed the Košice Program and became the first Minister of Defense. In the worst period of the "cult" he was demoted to accountant in a cooperative farm. In 1955 he became head of the Klement Gottwald Military Academy, and in April 1968, President of the Republic.

[6] Oldřich Černík, Prime Minister since April 1968, was born in the steel town of Ostrava, Moravia, in 1921. After working in the Vítkovice Steel mill he became a secretary in the regional Communist Party apparatus. From 1960–63 he was Minister of Fuels and Energy, and from 1963–68 was head of the Planning Commission. He is a graduate of the Ostrava School of Mining and Steel Engineering.

[7] One friend timed the meetings in his bureau. They lasted an average of 8 minutes, except when the boss came and the time jumped to 21 minutes. One branch secretary became so inventive in his false reports of meetings that the hierarchy came to seek the key to their success—and found that the branch had not met for a year!

television for the news. Editions of newspapers and political journals were snapped up as soon as they hit the stands. The readers now read first the political news and then turned to the sports page!

At the same time that the main developments were definitely strengthening socialism and renewing confidence in the Communist Party, some discordant voices were raised that tried to take advantage of free speech to express lack of confidence in the Party, and even a few who tried to recruit support for a return to capitalism. The most effective treatment for the latter was to let them talk and become known to the workers—who consistently repudiated them. In this way a number of reactionaries, even a few CIA agents, were exposed and rendered harmless.

There were also those who thought that the Communist Party had become so compromised by its past participation in illegal acts that it was hopeless to try to rehabilitate it. But again this was not a strong trend because the Party *had* taken the initiative in correcting its grave mistakes. The vast majority were solid for socialism, and convinced that the Party could regain its leading role. Many of these were impatient with the slow pace at which the removal of the guilty officials from positions of power was taking place. The new leadership did not want to perpetuate the old high-handed methods and inflict new injustices in the name of correcting old ones. The result was that no sweeping purge was carried out and a chorus of protest was raised against the delay.

As early as March 1968 the press was giving space to many such protests, but the most widely quoted, often as proof that the counterrevolution had taken over in Czechoslovakia, was the "Two Thousand Words" written by Ludvík Vaculík and endorsed by more than 70 intellectuals and workers. It was printed in *Literární listy* of June 27 and in three other papers—an amount of publicity which was itself criticized. It was a bitter, intemperate protest— but, if we remember the record of injustices still uncorrected, it is not too surprising. Since it is the main "proof" of "counterrevolution," let us examine it in some detail. The tenor of the 2,000 words may be judged from the following excerpts:

> Most of the nation accepted the program of socialism with hope. But the management of this program fell into the hands of the wrong people. It would not have been so bad that they did not

have enough experience with statesmanship, knowledge of facts or philosophical education, if they had had more of ordinary wisdom and the decency to let other more capable people gradually replace them.
The Communist Party, in which the people had great trust at the end of the war, gradually exchanged it for offices until it had them all and nothing else....
The unification of the Party with the state caused the Party to lose perspective.... The parliament forgot to discuss problems, the government forgot how to govern and the directors how to manage.

These were harsh terms, but even so the writers did not abandon the goal of socialism or even attempt to undermine the Communist Party as such. They continued:

First of all, we oppose the idea, if it appears, that a democratic revival can be accomplished without the Communists. This would be unjust and unreasonable as well. The Communists have established organizations; in these we must support the progressive wing. They have experienced functionaries, they have, after all, the decisive controls in their hands. They stand before the public with their Action Program, which is at the same time a program of the first rectifications of inequalities—and nobody else has any program as specific as it is.

The authors continue, stating that they are worried because the process of democratization was slowing down before all the needed laws and practical measures had been taken. The signers argued:

If we cannot expect anything more from the present central political organs, we have to achieve more in the districts and communities. Let us demand that those people leave who have misused their power, damaged public property, acted dishonestly or cruelly. We must find ways to make them leave. For example: public criticism, resolutions, demonstrations, strikes, collecting funds for their retirement and picketing their doors.

But they added:

We must reject any methods that are in conflict with the law, indecent or rude, because this could be used by those people [who had damaged public property, acted dishonestly or cruelly] to influence Alexander Dubček. . . . Let us support the Security police; it is not our intent to bring about a state of anarchy. Let us avoid quarrels with our neighbors, let us not get politically intoxicated.

This was no call to counterrevolution. But in uncommonly blunt words it did say why the signers thought that the process of cleansing the Party and government of those who had abused their power should not be stopped halfway. It is also significant that the signers had no organization. Nevertheless, many people in the leadership of the Party and government, while agreeing that the signers had the right to publish their ideas, also thought that it was an untimely document. The emphasis was too much on past mistakes, not enough on a positive program; but it was clearly for socialism, and most certainly not for a return to capitalism.

The "2,000 Words" were not only untimely, they were unfair to the new leadership. The document came just at the time when, as both First Secretary Dubček and Premier Oldřich Černík pointed out, fundamental progress was being made in correcting the errors and illegalities about which the signers were complaining. Both in the preparation of legislation in regard to rehabilitation and in review of Party programs and policies much intensive work was being done. The leaders of this review in the government and Party had long since passed from the stage of criticism typified by the "2,000 Words" to a recognition of the need for immediate action, not just in the economic sector but also in the political.

Furthermore, the progressive leadership was well aware of the dangers to socialism and to the Party that had arisen under the dictatorial era. Typical in this respect was the article in March of then Vice-Premier Černík in which he said:

> For many years it has been the tendency of the Party leadership to seclude itself in illusions about the unshakeable authority of the Party, about the boundless and constantly strengthening unity of the people and Party, about the farsightedness and almost infallibility of the leadership. . . . The Party was gradually being pushed to the brink of isolation. . . .
>
> A bold encounter with the facts and a drawing of realistic conclusions as a basis of the imminent process of rejuvenation of the Party and society was the substance of the debate and re-

sults of the December and January plenary sessions of the Central Committee of the Communist Party.

This realistic attitude towards facts and the resolute reckoning with false illusions, towards which some people are still casting their gaze, by no means implies that sight will be lost of the revolutionary aims and ideals of the Communist Party. On the contrary, this is the visible basis for gaining the real support of the broadest mass of the people. . . .

Our experiences have shown that in the coming epoch we shall be able to hold our ground in competition with advanced capitalist states only if we have a highly advanced socialist society, which makes full use of its advantages, of its internal profoundly democratic and humane character and which gives wide scope to the initiative, activity and creative self-assertion of all of its members.

(*Rudé právo*, March 14, 1968.)

The Action Program

The post-January 1968 leaders of the Czech and Slovak people were well aware that the complex and acute problems which they faced required thoroughgoing solutions. Patchwork of theory and practice would not be enough. A revolutionary advance in thinking and in action was essential. Josef Smrkovský,[8] one of the most popular and at the same time one of the most profound of the 1968 leaders, said:

It is necessary to deduce theoretical and practical conclusions from the fact that there no longer exist antagonistic classes in our country. We would be thrown backwards if we used—even

---

[8] Josef Smrkovský, born on February 20, 1911 in the village of Velenka, Central Bohemia, has held important posts in the Communist Party since he was 21. During the Nazi occupation he was active in the resistance. In May 1945 he organized the Prague uprising. After 1945 he was elected deputy chairman of the Czechoslovak National Council and after 1948 he became Deputy Minister of Agriculture, in charge of state farms. In 1951 he was arrested and imprisoned until 1955. He then became chairman of a cooperative farm. From 1963–65 he was Deputy Minister of Agriculture and Chairman of the Central Commission of People's Control and Statistics. In the new government formed in April 1968 he was Speaker of Parliament. In 1971 it was reported that he was dying of cancer in a Prague hospital.

though in another form—methods and means of the period of open struggle.

The Plenum of the Central Committee strove to find the causes of passivity and indifference to which we must no longer close our eyes. We became convinced that precisely what we had achieved in the reconstruction of society now facilitates and categorically requires a turn. A turn towards the democratization of the Party and of the whole of society, consistent and sincere, not weakened by any reservations but based on realistic and intelligible guarantees.

Therefore the Central Committee decided to work out a program of action, and to set to work on the project of development of socialist society, a program which will contain all well-tested practices, as well as the progressive local democratic traditions out of which our victory had been born. For our present tasks, and particularly for our road ahead, we shall find no ready-made patterns. It is up to us, Czechs and Slovaks, to set out courageously in unexplored terrain and to search in it for our Czechoslovak socialist road. *This is in fact our obligation to the entire international socialist movement.* This road leads us to solidify, all over again and anew, our unity with the Soviet Union and with all the socialist countries, doing so on the well-tested principles of equality. We shall establish a type of socialism that will have something to say even to Europe's industrial countries with their advanced revolutionary workers' movement.

Let us accord the past its due—truth, right, justice. Let us do so without delay, without sensationalism and recrimination, but consistently, so that we can concentrate on what is always the most important matter for Communists—the future.

(*Rudé právo,* February 9, 1968. Emphasis in original.)

This, not the "2,000 Words" or any antisocialist comment by individuals, was the spirit that characterized the period from January to August 1968. It is true that some people, both inside and outside of Czechoslovakia, may have had other ideas of what was going on here. But the main trend of thought among the leaders, and of the program of action they were working out, was in this spirit of revolutionary international socialism emphasized by Smrkovský. This was the kind of argument and appeal which won the support of the overwhelming part of the Czech and Slovak workers and intellectuals.

The political breakthrough at the December and January meetings of the Central Committee had been dramatic and even unexpected, since only a short time before the Novotný group had appeared to have firm control of the Party apparatus. The victory of the Dubček group meant that further political changes were possible, and since this was obviously an essential precondition for other advances the Central Committee concentrated a good deal of its attention upon its own internal reform. *Rudé právo,* official journal of the Party, summarized the conclusions of the Central Committee as follows:

> The Party as a whole and its organizations at all levels must apply their weight and exercise the leading role of the Party through the work of Communists active in organizations and institutions of state, economy and society, *not by outright directives. Direct Party control,* as experience has shown, interferes with actual management, curtails responsibility or takes it upon itself, and *is an expression of mistrust of the legally established authorities.* Such practices have been and still are the cause of the widespread tendency to look for alibis, and this is the root of many of our shortcomings in political morality. "Direct control" means also transferring the decision-making power to the party machine. Such a system risks curtailing democracy and the activities of elected bodies, and an increase of the anonymous character of management, and making plenary meetings a mere formality.
>
> (*Rudé právo,* February 8, 1968. My emphasis, G.W.)

Actually it was not a question of "risking" curtailing the activities of elected bodies—they had long since atrophied. Here the Party came up against a deep contradiction between fundamental democracy and its concept of the leading role of the party *combined with* "party discipline." The Czechoslovak Party wrestled with this problem, but had not solved it before the military intervention of August 1968 cut short all discussion of basic Party Policy. For example, First Secretary Dubček, in reporting on the Action Program to the Central Committee on April 1, 1968, remarked:

> Democracy does not mean never-ending conferences. The discussions and consultations must be followed by a conclusion binding for all members. . . . The principles of democratic centralism, which must be fully respected in intra-party life, and without which the Party would lose its capacity for action, requires the minority to submit to the conclusions, to the decisions of the majority, and to apply its opinion by adhering to intra-party rules.

Yet in the same speech Dubček also said:

> As regards the National Assembly (Parliament), we must fully ensure the application of the constitutional rights of this supreme state institution.

The ideas in those two paragraphs are strictly noncompatible.

In line with its leading role, the Communist Party usually (in the Novotný era always) takes up at Central Committee level all important legislation and appointments *before* they are submitted to the National Assembly. Since the Communist Party has the majority in the Assembly, this means that any program approved by the Central Committee, must, if "party discipline" continues to be binding, be automatically passed. The "debate" in parliament and in all local governmental bodies becomes sterile since it can change nothing. No matter what new arguments or facts are brought up the Party members are bound to a previously approved draft. In practice a small group such as the Presidium of the Party took over all legislative functions and, in the name of "democratic centralism," bound all members of the Party to that decision. This is the key to the atrophy of the elected bodies throughout the governmental structure. It is, in essence, as the Central Committee itself concluded in the above quotation, "an expression of mistrust of the legally established authorities." It is also an expression of mistrust of the Party membership itself. Sooner or later, the Party must choose between its goal of activating institutions like the National Assembly and the National Front and having them function in a democratic manner and the present Party rules which bind Party members in those institutions to previous Party decisions.

The concept of the "leading role of the Party" is clearly a key to the understanding of problems of socialist democracy and it is a problem to which Czechoslovak Party leaders devoted much thought. The Action Program sums up their ideas precisely—and it is a pity that it has been widely misquoted by those who would rather "prove" a point than be accurate. The Program has a special section headed: *"The leading role of the Party—a guarantee of socialist progress."* It begins by arguing that it is most important now that the Party *"justify"* its role, as it had been doing since January 1968. Then follows the much misquoted paragraph:

> In the past, the leading role of the Party was often conceived as a monopolistic concentration of power in the hands of Party bodies. This corresponds to the *false theory that the Party is the instrument of the dictatorship of the proletariat.* This harmful conception weakened the initiative and responsibility of the State, economic, and social institutions, damaged the Party's authority, and prevented it from carrying out its real functions. The Party's goal is not to become the universal "caretaker" of the society, to bind all organizations and every step taken in life by its directives. Its mission lies primarily in arousing socialist initiative, in showing the ways and actual possibilities of communist perspectives, and in winning over all workers to them through systematic persuasion, as well as by personal example.
> (*The Action Programme of the Communist Party of Czechoslovakia,* adopted by the Central Committee, April 5, 1968, ČTK English edition, p. 22.)

By quoting as a separate sentence only the italicized part some commentators have proven to their own satisfaction that the new Party leadership in Czechoslovakia was indeed counterrevolutionary. Actually, even out of context, the statement was quite correct for Czechoslovak conditions in 1968. *If the Party had identified its leading role with dictatorship of the proletariat in a period when class antagonisms had been overcome it would either have to liquidate itself—or maintain a dictatorship against the working class.* Instead of dogmatically continuing to repeat and apply a policy suitable for earlier eras and other countries, the Czechoslovak Party decided to expand and change its methods to those suitable to its country in an advanced stage of socialism. This, I submit, is not undermining the leading role of the Party. It is not counter-revolution.

The Action Program takes a firm theoretical position upon the issue of democracy and socialism. It reads:

After the 20th Congress of the Communist Party of the Soviet Union, which was an impulse for revival of the development of socialist democracy, the Party adopted several measures which were intended to overcome bureaucratic-centralist sectarian methods of management, to prevent the means of class struggle from being turned against the working people. Many Communists and whole working collectives tried to open the way to progressive development of the economy, the living standard, science and culture. The more definitely was class antagonism overcome and the foundations for socialism laid, the more urgent was the stress placed upon promotion of cooperation of all working people, of all social strata, groups and nationalities in Czechoslovakia and on fundamental changes in methods employed during the time of sharp class struggle. Furthermore, the development of socialist democracy was rightly seen as the main social condition for the realization of the humanist aims that are characteristic of socialism.

However, they met with lack of understanding, inhibitions and, in some cases, direct suppression. The survival of methods from the time of class struggle evoked an artificial tension among the social groups, nations and nationalities, between the generations, Communists and non-party people in this society. Dogmatic approaches impeded a full and timely reevaluation of the conceptions of the character of socialist construction.
(*Ibid.*, pp. 8–9.)

After the Action Program was submitted to the people for debate a lively discussion of both its political and economic provisions took place. Many suggestions were made for consideration at the 14th Congress of the Party scheduled to be held in the second week of September. Among these were such proposals as that the term of office of the First Secretary of the Party be strictly limited and that dual holding of office be eliminated. The discussion was made lively not just because of the importance of the problems but because the removal of censorship allowed the public to become much better informed. For the first time in years real criticism was possible and there was even the beginning of self-criticism. In the process of self-criticism and of listening to the voice of the people the Party rapidly recovered its prestige and could again assume a true leading role. In its *Report* of its May 29–June 1, 1968, meeting the Central Committee remarked: "Relying on the people, the Communists have widened the scope for democratic development. *This is why the Party continues to be the decisive force and the guarantee of this movement.*" (ČTK, translation, pp. 10–11. My emphasis. G.W.)

We should also note that for the first time in years active education against racism was going on. The Action Program said:

> The Party stresses that it will oppose all expressions of anti-Semitism, racism and any anti-humanist ideology, which would set the people against each other. (p. 17.)

The Action Program in its English translation is a 90-page document covering all aspects of social life. For example, two paragraphs of the section on the "Humanistic Mission of Culture" read:

> *It is necessary to overcome a narrowed understanding of the social and human function of culture and art, overestimation of their ideologicial and political role and underestimation of their basic general cultural and aesthetic tasks in the transformation of man and his world.*
> Socialist culture is one of the primary agents of penetration of socialist and humanist ideas in the world. *It helps unite the humanist streams of world culture. It has the capacity of bringing closer the socialist nations and of strengthening the cooperation and fraternal relations of nations and nationalities.* (pp. 80–81. Emphasis in original.)

The Action Program also proposed that democratic rights of free speech and assembly be ensured and that such specific rights as the freedom to travel abroad be *"precisely guaranteed by law."* In general the new program was directed toward a greater participation of the Czech and Slovak people in political life and toward a freer and richer cultural life. It was a program based on confidence in the political and intellectual maturity of the people, on their loyalty to socialism.

The Economic Program

The Action Program was not intended to be a finished blueprint for the reconstruction of political and economic life, but rather to serve as the basis for discussion and to give the people confidence that a thorough review of all problems was being undertaken which would result both in changes within the Party and in new legislation applicable to the general public. Previously when the Party was considering policy matters it had worked out all details at the top and then asked for the disciplined help of its officials and members in "selling" the program to the rest of the people. Here was a genuine effort to change this method so that the people actually had a voice in shaping the final new program.

The preliminary character of the program did not mean that its objectives were not clear, but rather that details had not been worked out, nor had all dilemmas and difficulties been solved. Not a few people were still seeking quick and simple solutions. Those who had worked most closely with the problems, and particularly with the economic problems, usually realized that no panaceas were available, and that in many cases it would be years before satisfactory readjustments and restructuring of the economy could be accomplished. As is typical among economists, even when they have the same general goal, there was much argument over interpretation of data and over the best methods to proceed. But there was no dispute that it was a splendid change to have access to essential data and to know that their ideas were being sought and heeded. The absence of dogmatic assertion and the revival of scientific analysis gave hope that, difficult though they were, the problems would be understood and new ways found to increase the efficiency of the economy.

The Action Program began its analysis of these economic problems with the recognition of the need for a creative development of the social system:

> Antagonistic classes no longer exist in our society and the main feature of internal development becomes the process of bringing all social groups closer together.
>
> Methods of management and organization hitherto used in the national economy are outdated and urgently demand changes, i.e., an economic system of management able to enforce a turn towards intensive growth.
>
> It will be necessary for our country to join in the world-wide scientific-technical revolution. This calls for particularly intensive cooperation of industrial and agricultural workers with the technical and specialized intelligentsia, and this will place high de-

The "New System"

mands upon the knowledge and qualifications of people and require the use of science.

A broad scope for social initiative, frank exchange of views and democratization of the whole social and political system becomes virtually the precondition for a dynamic socialist society, the basis upon which we will be able to hold our own in world competition and to fulfil our obligations towards the international working class movement. (pp. 7–8.)

The Central Committee continued with the direct acceptance of responsibility for the backward state of management:

Over the years difficulties piled up until they closed in a vicious circle. Subjective concepts . . . led to a precipitate expansion of heavy industry, to a disproportionate demand for labor power and raw materials and to expensive investments. This economic policy, enforced through directive administrative methods, no longer corresponds to the economic requirements and possibilities of our country and led to exhaustion of its material and human resources. Unrealistic tasks were placed upon the economy, illusory promises were made to the workers. . . .

These shortcomings were directly caused by the old system of management: Directives from the center replaced economic means, forms of supply and demand, and market relations. Socialist initiative did not grow. In economic life, independence, diligence, expertise and initiative were not appreciated, but instead, subservience, obedience and even kowtowing were rewarded.

A more profound reason for maintaining the obsolete methods of economic management were the deformations of the political system. Socialist democracy was not expanded in time, methods of revolutionary dictatorship deteriorated into bureaucracy and became an impediment to progress in all spheres of life. . . .

The main links in this chain were the remnants or reappearance of the bureaucratic, sectarian approach in the Party itself.
(*Action Program,* pp. 9–11.)

These are extensive quotations, but they are precise summaries of the main trend of public, official, and Party thinking in Czechoslovakia. The Action Program continued:

The main thing is to reform the whole political system so that it will permit the dynamic development of social relations, com-

bining broad democracy with a scientific, highly qualified management, strengthen the social order, stabilize socialist relations and maintain social discipline. (p. 28 Emphasis in original.)

We see that the leading body of the Communist Party repeatedly stressed the close link between the economic and the political changes necessary to socialist advance. This is the all-important difference from the programs of economic reform in other socialist countries. From their experience the Czechoslovak leaders had concluded that significant economic advance was not possible without fundamental political changes, changes which would alter the role of the Party, but strengthen it and socialism.

If we look at the specific *economic* changes suggested we will find that they do not differ radically from those already being practiced or being advocated in one or all of the neighboring socialist countries. Typical is the advocacy of decentralization of some of the powers of management and enhancing the role of the enterprise managers. In all countries this means some loosening of the ties that bind one enterprise to another in rigid producer-consumer relations, and some steps, timid or bold, in trying to activate the market as a substitute for *some* of the subjective and centralized decision-making. None of the other countries, and Czechoslovakia less than some others, goes as far as Yugoslavia in relying upon decentralized decision-making and response to market influences. Up to August 1968 no specific legislation had been proposed or adopted governing new market-management relations.

The Action Program was not only vague on this point, it was even somewhat contradictory in its assignments of powers of management:

The program of democratization of the economy *includes particularly the provision of ensuring the independence of enterprises* and enterprise groupings and their relative independence from state bodies, a full implementation of the right of the consumer to determine his consumption and style of life, the right to free choice of employment, the right and real possibility of different groups of working people and different social groups to formulate and defend their economic interests in shaping economic policy. (p. 50.)

The Action Program suggested that elected bodies within the enterprise participate in specific ways in management, somewhat in the manner of the workers' councils of 1945–48, with the trade unions playing a much more active role. At the same time the decentralization is subject to the overriding control of the State:

> Decision-making about the plan and the economic policy of the State must be a policy of mutual confrontation and harmonization of different interests—i.e., the enterprises, consumers, employees, different social groups in the population, nations, etc. —and a process of mutual combination of interest in long-term development of the economy and its immediate prosperity. Effective measures protecting the consumer against the abuse of monopoly position and economic power of production and trading enterprises are a necessary part of the activity of the State. The drafting of the national economic plan and national economic policy must be subject to the democratic control of the National Assembly, and specialized control by scientific institutions. The supreme body implementing the economic policy of the State is the Government. (pp. 56–57.)

This is a recognition of the need for more flexibility and democracy in decision-making, but it still provides for sufficient centralized power to protect essential social interests. It will take much experimentation and many years to find desirable balances between the need for decentralization and the need for social controls.

The First Results

In the short time from the publication of the Action Program and the formation of the new government in April until August, it was not possible to put much of the program into effect, but some significant steps were taken. For example, the new Minister of Interior, Josef Pavel,[9] was doing a remarkable job of removing from

---

[9] Josef Pavel, born September 18, 1908 near České Budějovice, joined the Komsomols in 1929 and the Communist Party in 1932. From 1935–37 he studied at the International Lenin School in Moscow and at the Army School in Riazin; in 1937–38 was commander of the Czechoslovak volunteers in Spain, later captured and interned in France and North Africa. From 1943–45 he fought with Czech forces in the West. In 1946–47 First Secretary of the Communist Party in Pilsen. In 1948 appointed the first commander of the People's Militia. From January 1949 to March he was deputy Minister of Interior in charge of police and border guards. Resigned in protest at intrusion of secret police into his jurisdiction. Arrested in 1951 he was held three years without trial and then sentenced to 25 years in prison as an "agent of the West." The Czechoslovak Supreme Court ordered his release on October 22, 1955. After his release he worked in a sports organization until appointed Minister of Interior in April 1968.

their positions police officials who had participated in the torture of prisoners or committed other illegalities. Some 200 were tried and dismissed. But the main change was the return of the Ministry of Interior to the legal relationship of authority:

> So far as the organization of the Ministry is concerned, it will be directly subordinated to the government, namely to the Prime Minister. "We have changed the Ministry," Minister Pavel said, "into a policy-making and control body. . . . Special attention is being devoted to the removal of certain operations from the competence of the Ministry in an attempt to cut down the huge apparatus."
> (*Pragopress Bulletin* No. 16, May 20, 1968, p. 7.)

This meant that the Party would no longer exercise *direct* control over the *daily* operations of the Ministry—but of course Pavel and most of the other top executives of the Ministry were Communists. This pullback of the Party from direct performance of governmental functions was one of the aspects of the Action Program most opposed by the Parties in other socialist countries, and shortly after the arrival of the troops on August 21 Pavel was forced to resign.

One of the hopes of the capitalists and fears of many socialists in the period after January 1968 was that Czechoslovakia would break her alliance with the socialist countries and "turn to the West." The Czechoslovak Party and government repeatedly rejected this idea in the most explicit language. The Action Program says:

> *We stand resolutely on the side of progress, democracy and socialism in the struggle of the socialist and democratic forces against the aggressive attempts of world imperialism.* (p. 84, Emphasis in original.)

Speaking in Slovakia on May 23, 1968, President Svoboda said:

> Our society is, and will remain, socialist. But we seek a consistent democratization of our whole political and social system, in which citizens of this country will have equal rights and duties not only on paper but in fact. . . . Our friendship and alliance with the Soviet Union is firm and enduring.
> (*Práce,* Prague, May 24, 1968.)

The then Foreign Minister, Jiří Hájek,[10] repeatedly emphasized the economic, geographic, and political as well as military reasons for this alliance with the Soviet Union and the neighboring socialist countries. He took the principled position that the Czechoslovak Government would not renew diplomatic relations with West Germany until it explicitly recognized the present boundaries of the states of Europe and repudiated as invalid, from the beginning, the Munich agreement. In Moscow at the end of April he recalled the many times that the Soviet Union had assisted Czechoslovakia and then said:

> There are elements trying to cast a shadow over Soviet-Czechoslovak friendship. But they will never succeed in shaking it. . . . The voice of Czechoslovakia has always been the voice of a member of the socialist community of nations. . . . Our basic policy orientation remains unchanged.
> (*New Times,* Moscow, May 1, 1968.)

As we have said, political and economic problems of many kinds were demanding solution, and by August 1968 only tentative and partial solutions had been found for most of them. The most encouraging thing was the frank recognition of the importance of such problems and a return to scientific methods of seeking solutions for them. Josef Špaček,[11] a member of the Party Presidium, remarked:

> We had been retreating from Marxism. A dogmatic revision of Marxism was being enforced, denying the specific historical approach toward the solution of all problems connected with the building of socialism. There was a failure to realize that Marxism was not a dogma, but a guide of action. The criticism of the Stalinist cult in the mid-1950s did not go deep enough to recognize this fundamental fact. Thus it frequently happened that the

---

[10] Jiří Hájek, born in 1913 near Benešov, Bohemia, was imprisoned during the Nazi occupation. Talented linguist, Corresponding Member of the Academy of Sciences, historian and Professor of the College of Politics and Economics, a diplomat, for many years Czechoslovak ambassador to the United Nations and Great Britain, from 1965–67 Minister of Education, in April 1968 he became Foreign Minister. After being forced out of the government he returned to his work in the Academy of Sciences.

[11] Josef Špaček, born August 7, 1927 near Kutná Hora; from 1946–47 district secretary of Union of Czechoslovak Youth, from 1947–66 a district Party functionary; member of the Central Committee of the Party, and a member of the Presidium during the reform period.

very efforts to revive Marxist political thinking, to comprehend a new form of the leading role of the Party and to change the whole style and system of political leadership of society, were branded as revisionism of Marxism. It is necessary to overcome these deformations, otherwise we shall again and again fall victims of the schematicism which we have renounced. That requires, however, a much more intensive development of creative Marxist theoretical and political thinking. We will not be able to hold our ground in competition with non-Marxist theories and ideologies, if we do not succeed in accomplishing a fundamental change in this respect.
(Discussion at the Plenary Session of the Central Committee, *Pragopress Bulletin* No. 12/14, May 6, 1968, p. 55.)

Such was the quality of the men leading Czechoslovakia after January 1968. This quality of leadership was born of the high political maturity of the Czech and Slovak people. The leaders were articulating the demands of the workers and farmers and intellectuals of their country for bold advances in socialist thinking and in the organization of socialist society. It is this deep-rooted understanding of the dialectics of change which gave the reform movement in Czechoslovakia its firm political strength.

CHAPTER 8

The Intervention

It is quite remarkable that all during the Novotný regime—when a highly centralized bureaucracy was abusing socialist legality, when it was increasingly evident that the Czechoslovak economy was being mismanaged in a serious way, when the prestige of the top Party leadership had dropped so low that they could no longer lead but only dictate, and when this situation was discrediting socialism itself—no protests were made by the neighboring socialist countries. On the contrary, relations were most cordial and mutually laudatory.

In contrast, when in January 1968 the Czechoslovak Party led its members and the people of both nations in an extraordinary breakthrough that overcame that tight dictatorial bureaucracy, when the Party began to regenerate itself, and formulated the outlines of a program to put the management of the economy on a scientific and efficient basis, when it began to restore socialist legality in all spheres of society, when it began a reexamination of obsolete dogma and a return to dialectical materialist concepts of development of society—to Marxism not as dogma but as a theory of action—in short, when the Czechoslovak people were able, belatedly, to move ahead to a higher stage of democratic, humanist socialism, then, and only then, did some of the top Party officials of other socialist countries show alarm.

After January 1968, although the new system of management was only in its first experimental stage, the economy began to perform more efficiently. At the end of the first six months productivity per worker was six percent above June 1967, real wages were also six percent higher, and the supply of consumer goods was 13 percent higher—a good indication that inflation was being brought under control. Furthermore, as we have said, most of the economic elements of the "new system," such as greater independence for the enterprises, were either in effect in the neighboring socialist countries, or being advocated by their more responsible economists and administrators. We must look elsewhere for the reasons for intervention.

It was the Czechoslovak program for change in the area of political economy, such as the proposal to do away with the complete monopolization of foreign trade, and the strictly political measures, such as the reform of Party rules, which were the cause of alarm. Here the measures being considered strengthened socialism by making it more efficient, by removing specific roadblocks to scientific and technological advance, yet retaining or restoring the essential features of socialism. For example, there was *no* legislation being considered that would make possible the restoration of capitalist ownership of industry and the exploitation of workers. Instead, direct participation of the workers in management was increased, but with safeguards for the general social interest.

All charges that the Czechoslovak Government was toying with a return to capitalism were either wishful thinking on the part of the capitalist press, or deliberate misrepresentation. As just one example of this, let us take the charge that the then Deputy Premier and leading economist, Ota Šik, was advocating the restoration of private enterprise. Yuri Zhukov, in an article in *Pravda* (Moscow) of July 26, 1968 wrote:

> Practical actions in Prague speak for themselves. One of the leading officials, O. Šik, spoke on television asking for "encouragement for developing middle and small private business."

In order to get the words for that short sentence Zhukov used parts of three paragraphs of Šik's actual television speech. In his reply in *Rudé právo* of July 28, Šik quoted what he had said in regard to the problem of services and small-scale production:

> I do not see any reason why, let us say, a few (e.g., 4 to 10) skilled citizens could not form *cooperatives* either of producers or artisans.

Šik's only reference to middle-size private business was to those *now existing in the German Democratic Republic*. Zhukov's article was widely reprinted as proof that important government officials in Czechoslovakia were counterrevolutionary. *No correction was ever printed by* Pravda *or any other of the papers that had used the original story*. The result of these misrepresentations was that many people, who had a sincere interest in the development of socialism, obtained a completely inaccurate picture of what was taking place in Czechoslovakia.

On March 23, 1968, First Secretary of the Czechoslovak Communist Party, Alexander Dubček, was invited to Dresden. There he was lectured on the alleged dangers of the new course of development in Prague. He defended not only the right of the Czechoslovak people to determine their own development, but also the correctness of the specific socialist road that they had taken.

The Warsaw-Brezhnev Doctrine

Within Czechoslovakia there was increasing apprehension that the mounting attack in the press and radio of some of the Warsaw Pact countries might mean some form of direct intervention to cut short economic and political changes. This concern became acute as the previously scheduled maneuvers of the Warsaw Pact troops were inexplicably prolonged—the foreign troops just could not seem to find their way back out of the country! Then, on July 18, 1968, the Communist Party leaders of the Soviet Union, East Germany, Poland, Hungary, and Bulgaria meeting in Warsaw issued a letter that asserted the right of those countries to intervene in Czechoslovakia, if in their judgment this became necessary to protect socialism. The letter is long and declarative, but it must be studied since it sets out a doctrine that is of utmost importance to the development of the world socialist movement. Its most important paragraphs read:

> The development of events in your country deeply disquiets us. The rise of reaction against your Party and the bases of the social system in Czechoslovakia, supported by imperialism, threatens to lead your country away from the path of socialism and, as a consequence, is a danger to the interests of the whole socialist system. . . .
> We have no intention to intervene in such matters as are the purely internal concern of the Party and your state, to violate the principle of independence and equality in relations among Communist parties and socialist countries.
> We are not appearing before you as representatives of yesterday who are trying to prevent you from correcting shortcomings, that is, the violations of socialist justice that have occurred.

We are not interfering in the methods of planning a socialist national system of the economy of Czechoslovakia, in your measures that are directed at improving the structure of the economy, for the development of socialist democracy.

Not one bit of proof was given that any "rise of reaction" had taken place in Czechoslovakia, unless a reference to the "2,000 Words" or unsubstantiated references, without even dates or names, to "a number of organs of mass information that are systematically carrying on a real moral terror [against the Novotný group]" are regarded as proof. The men who had shared responsibility for the illegal acts against and imprisonment of 70,000 victims, with the execution of 178, now whined for mercy when they were retired on a double pension! The reassurances of "noninterference" were all the more disquieting because they were followed by the assertion that:

At the same time *we cannot consent* to hostile forces forcing your country from the socialist path and creating the threat of tearing Czechoslovakia away from the socialist commonwealth. *This is no longer your concern alone.* . . . There has arisen a situation which is absolutely unacceptable for a socialist country. . . . *The entire course of events in the last few months* in your country show that the forces of counterrevolution, supported by imperialist centers, have waged a broad attack against the socialist system and have not run against opposition of the Party and popular power. . . . *A determined fight to maintain the socialist system in Czechoslovakia is not only your, but also our task.* (My emphasis. G.W.)

It is curious that while the Party leaders who signed this letter condemned "the entire course of events" in Czechoslovakia they had almost no specific proposals *except for the reimposition of censorship.* This, as we have seen, had nothing to do with national security, but a great deal to do with protecting bureaucrats from exposure and criticism. The letter did demand the "stopping of all political organizations that speak against socialism"—but this did not apply to any existing political organization, except *perhaps* that of the former political prisoners, "Club 231." Club 231 was impatient in its demands and some foreign agents were found in it. But was it a serious threat to socialism? Certainly the government and Party remained in complete control at all times. There were no riots, and the only demonstrations were in support of the government. The entire country was peaceful. It had not even been necessary to call out the police—let alone the army and militia.

This warning letter was the more ominous for Czechoslovakia because it substituted the prejudiced judgment of these non-elected foreign groups for the considered opinion not only of the Czechoslovak Parliament, but also of the new Party majority led by Dubček. All of the representative bodies in Czechoslovakia immediately replied, rejecting the Warsaw interpretation of events.

On July 19 the Central Committee of the Communist Party of Czechoslovakia met and issued a resolution fully supporting the "principled stand and prudence" of Dubček and the other party and government leaders. Its reply to the Warsaw letter was firm yet conciliatory:

> Guided by international tradition and the principles of Marxism-Leninism, the Central Committee is profoundly aware of the responsibility for the fate of socialism in our country, not only to its own people, but also to the Communist movement. The basis of its procedure is, and will continue to be, the solution of our national tasks and needs, respecting the interests and goals of socialist countries and progressive forces of the world. The Central Committee considers the ties and cooperation with the Soviet Union and the other socialist countries to be the permanent international framework of socialist development of Czechoslovakia. . . .

On the same same day the Presidium of the National Front headed by Dr. František Kriegel,[1] made a declaration which began:

---

[1] František Kriegel, born April 10, 1908 in Stanislawow, Poland, was active in the revolutionary youth movement there and not permitted to study medicine. He came to Prague and was graduated from the Faculty of Medicine, Charles University, in 1934. From 1936–39 he was a medical doctor with the international Brigade in Spain. In 1939 he was put in a concentration camp in France. From 1945–49 a member of the Presidium of the Regional Committee of the Central Committee in Prague and Deputy Commander of the People's Militia. From 1949–59 Deputy Minister of Health. 1960–63 medical adviser in Cuba. From 1964–65 head of a research institute for rheumatism; in 1966 member of the Central Committee of the Communist Party; from April 4, 1968 to August 31, a member of the Presidium and Chairman of the Central Committee of the National Front. He was forced to resign by the intervening forces.

Citizens of Czechoslovakia! All nations have moments of greatness in their history which are of key importance for their further development. Precisely at this time the people of Czechoslovakia are going through a period that is a great opportunity for socialism, that opens the gates to socialism and democracy. These two ideas are inseparably connected with the best traditions of our nations. . . .

We express our conviction that the decision on the future of our society, on the form of socialism in Czechoslovakia, is a sovereign matter of our people. They must determine and choose their own way of life, they must decide the future of our Republic. Their maturity, shown by their behavior throughout this year, is a guarantee that we shall not stray from the socialist path, that counterrevolution of any kind will find no fertile ground in our Republic. The positive attitude of our people toward socialism is founded on their deep sense of justice and right, their democratic feeling.

The fundamental civil rights such as freedom of speech, of assembly and association, which have revived in our country, are integrally linked with the needs of our people, their ways of thinking and their life. There can be no doubt that our people can use these rights for the benefit of our nations for progress and socialism.

(*Rudé právo,* July 19, 1968.)

This was the voice of courageous leaders of a small country appealing to rationality, for the sovereign rights of their people. The Warsaw letter, by asserting the duty of the Party leaders of the Soviet Union and associated countries to determine on their own whether Czechoslovakia was following socialist policies and to intervene in any manner they thought effective, proclaimed a doctrine, now commonly known as the "Brezhnev doctrine," highly dangerous to the world socialist movement. It is the application to relations among the socialist countries of the old imperialist doctrine that capitalism can intervene in any country to protect its interests. Used to justify the United States intervention in such areas as Vietnam and the Dominican Republic, the doctrine was clever, since capitalism is engaged in a holding operation, in an attempt to preserve the *status quo*. It is a doctrine that sets aside all international law and treaties, including the United Nations, if and when a powerful nation decides that its interests will be advanced by such use of force.

Quite aside from fundamental legality and morality, the doctrine is not suitable for socialism since socialism is an expanding form of social and productive relations. Yet if any country turned to socialism, it might under the Warsaw-Brezhnev doctrine, lose its sovereignty to the most powerful socialist nation. Any concerned political leader might hesitate, therefore, to permit his country to turn to socialism, and extending socialism becomes much more difficult. It is also a certain way to increase international conflicts since there is more than one center of socialist power. Should China, if and when she has the power, have the right to invade the Soviet Union to stamp out the counterrevolution which, its leaders assert, is rampant there?

The apprehension with which the Czechoslovak people regarded the Warsaw letter doctrine was intensified by the fact that the troops of the Warsaw Pact countries remained on Czechoslovak territory long after their scheduled spring maneuvers had ended. At the same time the press and radio attacks on Czechoslovakia sharply increased in those countries. Amid this heightened tension the leaders of the Czechoslovak and Soviet Communist parties met on July 29 at Čierná nad Tisou on the border of Eastern Slovakia and, after very difficult bargaining, agreement was reached. The other signers of the Warsaw letter were then summoned to Bratislava, where on August 3 the Bratislava Agreement was signed by the Party leaders of Czechoslovakia, the Soviet Union, the German Democratic Republic, Poland, Hungary, and Bulgaria.

That agreement, aside from a routine polemic against imperialism, contained assurance that the Communist Parties were seeking "ways of strengthening and promoting fraternal cooperation of the socialist countries." Among the most important paragraphs were the following:

> Experience has convinced the brother parties that they can advance along the socialist road only if they are strictly and consistently guided by the general laws of bulding socialist society and, first of all, by enhancing the leading role of the working class and its vanguard the Communist parties. In doing so, each fraternal party takes into account national peculiarities and con-

ditions, as it creatively solves the problems of socialist development. . . .

The participants of the conference expressed their firm resolve to do all in their power in order to deepen all-round cooperation on the principles of equality, respect for sovereignty and national independence, territorial integrity, fraternal mutual assistance and solidarity.

(Text as given by the *World Marxist Review,* September 1968, p. 3. My emphasis. G.W.)

With these assurances and with the departure of the Warsaw Pact troops from Czechoslovakia, the tension eased and the people turned to the ardent but completely peaceful discussion of policies and problems to be considered at the 14th Congress of the Czechoslovak Communist Party scheduled to begin on September 9. There was a new enthusiasm for socialism, a new strength for the government but, and this was what concerned Brezhnev and the others, the discussion continued to reconsider the role of the Communist Party. The intent was to change it from a dictatorial to a truly *leading* role. Then, near midnight on August 20, 1968, with no previous warning, the troops of the Soviet Union, East Germany, Poland, Hungary, and Bulgaria entered Czechoslovakia. The official explanation was:

> Tass is authorized to state that party and government leaders of the Czechoslovak Socialist Republic have asked the Soviet Union and other allied states to render the fraternal Czechoslovak people urgent assistance, including assistance with armed forces.
>
> (*Tass,* Moscow, August 21, 1968.)

CHAPTER 9

Aftermath – But No Epitath

With the intervention began a bizarre time about which it is not yet possible to make a full scientific report, in part because the first concession forced from the Czechoslovak representatives was that all negotiations would be secret and only such reports of them could be made public as were agreed to by the Soviet Union. Any criticism, even referring to the invading troops as "occupation forces," is regarded as an unfriendly act and a proof that conditions in Czechoslovakia have not returned to normal—and the troops are to stay until their commanders decide that conditions *are* normal.

One important characteristic of the period after August 21 is that the flow of information has been cut down and distorted. As one example let us take the Tass announcement quoted just above. When, shortly after the intervention, the then Czechoslovak Foreign Minister Jiří Hájek in most restrained language told the United Nations Security Council that no responsible persons had issued such an invitation (and only the Parliament had the power to do so) he was savagely attacked in *Izevestia* of September 3, 1968. *Izvestia* charged Minister Hájek with having changed his name from Karpeles and with having collaborated with the Gestapo. Actually this was the revival of an old file that Beria had used against *Bedřich* Hájek in the 1950s. As a result of that charge Bedřich Hájek had served five years in prison before his friends could prove to the courts that he had been in England at the time Beria charged him with collaborating with the Gestapo in Prague. *Izvestia* was therefore using a false charge against a different man to attack the Foreign Minister of another socialist country. The irony of this action was that they succeeded in forcing Jiří Hájek to resign even though all the people in Czechoslovakia knew that he had a long record of anti-Nazi resistance, that he had been arrested by the Gestapo on September 30, 1940, and sentenced to 12 years in prison. Despite all protests from the Czechoslovak Party and Government, *neither Izvestia nor any other paper in any of the five Warsaw-letter countries ever printed a correction.* The false accusations are still being reprinted in countries as far away as South America.

The timing of the intervention indicates that a primary purpose was to prevent the holding of the 14th Congress of the Czechoslovak Communist Party scheduled to begin on September 9, 1968. This halted the reform of the Party and the removal of the main officials who had lost the confidence of the members. The intervention, nominally to insure the "leading role" of the Party, has crippled it by denying it the right to function in a normal way, by insisting that officials remain in office who no longer dared to appear in the factories they had once represented. Because of this the workers first turned more to the trade unions to represent them even in their political demands, and then lapsed into apathy.

The disposition of the troops indicated that there was no real fear of intervention by any capitalist country. The troops only belatedly and in token force approached the western frontiers—they were concentrated in the interior cities. The first acts were not to protect, but to arrest leading Party and government officials. The tanks were around the Party headquarters, the Parliament, the means of communication, the Academy of Science. Guns were massed against ideas. One of the first orders issued was the following:

> I, representative of the armies of the Warsaw Agreement, First Lieutenant Orlov, Yuri Alexandrovitch, order all the workers and members of the Presidium of the Czechoslovak Academy of Sciences to stop their work on August 22 before 13:00 o'clock, and to vacate all the buildings of the Academy of Sciences of the Czechoslovak Socialist Republic.
> Signed:

Yet the Warsaw letter and the Bratislava Agreement had each professed a respect for national sovereignty and that they had no intention at all of intervening in the internal affairs of Czechoslovakia.

The conflict between professed purpose and actual behavior is illustrated by the fact that in the Warsaw-agreement countries a whole campaign of sympathy was built up for the Czechoslovak People's Militia—yet one of the first acts of the intervening armies was to confiscate the arms of the militia wherever they could find them and to display them to the world as arms of counterrevolutionaries! The militia had needed no outside defense, and overwhelmingly supported the Dubček party policies and the government headed by Oldřich Černík. Further, the three main founders of the militia (and still highly respected by them), Josef Pavel, František Kriegel, and Josef Smrkovský,[1] have all been repeatedly attacked by the intervening powers, and have been forced out of office.

Vladimír Mináč, writer and member of the Central Committee,[2] speaking *before* the intervention, quite prophetically summed up the attitude of the Czech and Slovak people:

> The complications and difficulties stemming from the battle of ideas were to be expected and so I am not surprised. Those who sigh and complain understand nothing. It will not be comfortable to be a Communist.
>
> Every thought of ours must be just, every argument truthful. Those who have in their briefcases only a few phrases, and who think that all they need to do is to add a few new post-January ones, will not get along because the issue is not only a change of positions, but a change of attitude towards reality, society and the historical development of socialism.
>
> Let nothing deter us from this immense task; not the misgivings of some, or the shouts of others. If we have faith in the grandeur of man, in the possibility of his nobility, if we esteem our Czech and Slovak nations, if we believe in their inner need for justice, we must with all our strength help to move society towards freedom and towards truth, with wisdom and deliberation, but uncompromisingly.
>
> (*Pragopress Bulletin,* No. 8/10, April 22, 1968.)

The invasion resulted in comparatively little physical damage or loss of life. One American tourist looking at the burned-out

---

[1] When the leadership of the Communist Party established the People's Militia in 1948 it appointed Josef Pavel as the first commander, with Dr. Kriegel as his deputy, and Josef Smrkovský as the political commissar.
(*Rudé právo,* February 25, 1969.)

[2] Vladimír Mináč, born February 2, 1922 near Rimavská Sobota, Slovakia. Took part in the Slovak Uprising (1944–45), was captured and sent to a concentration camp. From 1945–46 editor of the army paper *Obrana lidu;* from 1950–51 Secretary of the Union of Slovak Writers; from 1951–65 editor and screenwriter; in 1968 member of the Central Committee of the Communist Party.

apartment houses and the bullet-riddled National Museum remarked: "Hell! One good riot produces more damage back home." That misses the point entirely. The damage was not in physical property or lives lost, but in the crushing of the highest of human aspirations. This was a blow not only to the Czechoslovak people, but to the hopes of people around the world that socialism could lead the way to a higher form of human relations, a society freed from the insecurities, anxieties, and inequalities of capitalism and from the dictatorial methods, restrictions of freedom, and bureaucratic petty tutelage of the first overcentralized model of socialism.

The demonstration that Czechoslovakia could achieve a socialism that was both democratic and more efficient would have been an inspiration for millions of people all around the world. The crushing of those aspirations leaves us with only the stubborn conviction that the same forces that gave rise to the changes in Czechoslovakia will eventually force changes in the invading countries. This is a terrible letdown from the high hopes of the spring of 1968, but it is not an entirely unrealistic optimism. Already two of the leaders most eager for the intervention, Ulbricht of East Germany and Gomulka of Poland, have fallen as a result of the need for internal changes within their own countries—changes in the direction the Czechoslovaks advocated.

Within Czechoslovakia the political and social situation is grim. Practically nothing remains of the reforms introduced in 1968: censorship is back in more drastic form than ever; even distinguished citizens are not permitted to travel abroad—only those who are a trusted part of the apparatus; all of the old police, thrown out by Pavel because of their illegal activities, are back on the job and enjoying their power to the full; plays and films are censored and drab. Orchestras and theaters, including the world-famous Dívadlo za Branou (Theater Behind the Gate, closed June 1972) have been shut down or denied travel abroad. Many of the best directors, such as Ota Krejča, are out of jobs and some out of the country.

The newspapers and journals are filled with dogma from third-rate minds. The bitter farce of the less educated Party members presuming to lead the Academy of Sciences, most of whose members are also in the Party, is being re-enacted. At the 29th General Assembly of the Academy on March 9, 1972, the members went through the motions of instructing their presidium to "consistently enforce the leading role of the Party in science." The Parliament and other elected bodies have relapsed into the coma of the Novotný period. All of the most effective leaders have been removed from public life: Smrkovský, Hájek, Pavel, Kriegel, Goldstücker, Cisař, Šik, and hundreds of others down to the level of the factories. The people, from students to coal heavers, are apathetic and many are cynical. What, now, is the point of resistance? Overt acts only give excuses to prolong the occupation, and economic sabotage will hurt only the Czechoslovak people. The country is simply too small for effective resistance against the giant that dictates to them. Outsiders who advise heroics might have second thoughts if they were Czechs or Slovaks.

The people of Czechoslovakia now have no choice in their officials. Men like Alois Indra and Vasil Bilák, who now claim to have invited the occupiers, are regarded as traitors and despised by the overwhelming majority of the Czechoslovak people, yet they presume to lecture other socialist countries on morality and economic policy. One of the last of the real leaders to be forced out of office was First Secretary of the Communist Party, Alexander Dubček, who had to resign on April 17, 1969. He was replaced by Dr. Gustav Hušak.[1]

How bleak are the immediate prospects may be judged from the tone of Hušak's acceptance speech:

> I have said, and Comrade President Svoboda has mentioned in his speech, that for nearly a year we have not been able to get out of our critical situation. Top organs of our Party and state have repeatedly explained the causes of this to the people and the ways out of the crisis by a calming down so that we can get to the solution of the most urgent problems of our working peo-

---

[1] Gustav Hušak, born in 1913 near Bratislava, is a graduate of the law faculty of the Comenius University of Bratislava. From 1938 to 1943 he worked in a legal office. From 1943 on he was active in the illegal Communist Party work and played a leading role in the Slovak Uprising, for which he received many decorations. In 1945 he became Slovak Commissioner for Transport and Technology. From 1946–50 he was Chairman of the Board of Commissioners as well as holding other offices. In 1945 and from 1949–51 he was a member of the Central Committee of the Party. In 1951 he was arrested on charges of "Slovak Nationalism" and imprisoned until 1960. For three years he worked in a construction enterprise, and then, until 1968, he worked in the Academy of Sciences. In April 1968 he became Deputy Prime Minister.

ple, so that our state may live, if one can put it this way, normally in its internal and external relations. . . . (*Rudé právo,* April 18, 1969.)

Here is posed one of the basic questions confronting the world —the right of small nation-states to live, to attain and maintain true sovereignty. That right is put in jeopardy by two different forces: the difficulty of small countries to develop and use efficiently modern large-scale technologies, and the tendency of powerful nations to assume that they have the right and duty to impose their policies on the weak. True, this imposition of policies usually takes the form of a coerced signature or "invitation" of occupation by unauthorized puppets. It makes no practical difference that such signatures or invitations have no standing in international law.

One conjunction of these two forces can be seen in the Soviet concept of the future "integrated" development of the countries in the Council for Mutual Economic Assistance (CMEA or COMECON). At the 24th Congress of the Soviet Communist Party, Leonid Brezhnev argued:

> The economic integration of the socialist countries is a new and complex process. It implies a new and broader approach to many economic questions, and the ability to find the most rational solutions, meeting *the interests not only of the given country but of all cooperating participants. (Pravda,* October 27, 1971. My emphasis, G.W.)

This could be subject to quite a reasonable interpretation, but it is also precariously close to extending to the economic sphere the political concepts of the Warsaw-Brezhnev doctrine: "this is not your concern alone." This becomes more ominous when read in context with other articles relating to the problems of "integration" of the CMEA countries. For example, Y. Kormnov, wrote:

> International specialization and cooperation of production are *all-embracing* forms of cooperation covering *all* spheres of socialist reproduction: Production, distribution, exchange and consumption, and also natural, scientific, technological, organizational and legal prerequisites. (*Voprosy Ekonomiki,* No. 8, 1971. My emphasis. G.W.)

This might not leave much room for national sovereignty. Lenin, who had caustic comments about great-nation chauvinism and who did much to advance the concept of national rights, is now being quoted, out of context, as justification for the idea that if the CMEA countries are to develop their mutual trade they must also integrate their planning and economic management and, in the end, give up their sovereignty. As one of many such articles, let us cite that of Y. T. Usenko, Doctor of Juridical Sciences, "Essence and Principles of Socialist Economic Integration," in which he argues that "promoting socialist economic integration" among the CMEA countries is of "paramount importance." He then quotes Lenin:

> The aim of socialism is not only to end the division of mankind into tiny states and the isolation of nations in any form, it is not only to bring nations closer together, it is to integrate them. *(Sovetskoye Gosudarstvo i Pravo,* No. 11, 1971, *Collected Works* [Moscow] Vol. 22, p. 146.)

Lenin, of course, was speaking of an advanced stage of socialist development. He cannot properly be quoted to justify use of economic, political, and even military pressures on small countries to "integrate," that is, to conform to the ideas of the strongest power in regard to social and economic organization, planning, and management. One can understand that, on reading and hearing such a propaganda campaign, the Czechoslovak people do not anticipate an immediate withdrawal of the occupying forces. That must await internal changes and democratization within the Soviet Union itself.

Conclusion

Starting with the inevitability of change, from the fact that for the foreseeable future we must expect great advances in science and the technology, we know that many complex new economic and social problems will arise. These are not just problems of production, of pollution of the environment and depletion of natural resources, but those relating to economic and political power, to distribution of incomes, ownership of the means of production, to medical care, poverty, unemployment and inflation, efficiency of transport, monopolies and competition, incentives for work, bureaucracy, individual liberties, and much else. Often these problems are acutely frustrating and there is a persistent tendency to seek simple panaceas. But there are no easy solutions for many of the dilemmas of high-technology and large-scale production complexes. Today, with both national competition and that between capitalism and socialism, no society can rest content with the *status quo* and long survive. It must move on to greater efficiency, more acceptable standards of living, more effective democracy or it will perish. This situation will continue at least as long as we have competition between capitalism and socialism.

This conclusion differs drastically from that of the ecologists who, properly alarmed at problems of pollution, exhaustion of resources, and increasing population, seek to turn back the clock, to curb technological change and even to reduce by as much as fifty percent the gross national product of advanced countries such as the United States. (See the articles in *Economic Growth vs. the Environment,* edited by W. A. Johnson and John Hardesty, Wadsworth Publishing Co., Belmont, California, 1971.) While one may sympathize with the fears of the ecologists, the solutions they propose are often unrealistic. They fail to see, for example, that the only countries that have the zero population growth that they advocate are those with high technologies and high standards of living. Some ecologists emphasize the need to change our goals in regard to living standards and the necessity to recycle materials, and some even recognize the need to modify our economic systems. They fail to see that what is needed is a combination of these changes and new technologies. Take the example of paper consumption and the pollution caused by paper mills together with the destruction of our forests. Recycling of paper, the reduction of advertising and excessive packaging, and the use of nylon or other reuseable shopping bags would all help. But *also* essential is the reduction of polluting effluents from the paper mills, and this can come only through further advances in technology and the application of known pollution controls through further investments.

A major fallacy is that "All power pollutes." (*Ibid.* p. 30.) With advances in technology, nonpolluting sources of power, the tides, winds, sun, and geothermal heat could all be used with minimal pollution. If thermonuclear power could be harnessed, that would also be essentially nonpolluting. The solution of the power problem is essentially a matter of altering national priorities for investment, and once the problem of nonpolluting and nonexhaustible power is solved, many of the other problems that worry the ecologists and which should worry all of us, can also be solved. The relevant point here is that such developments in technology and the related changes in social goals and social systems may not be compatible with the capitalist ethic and the capitalist system. They are certainly not feasible through the uncontrolled action of the market. The profit motive and the uninformed and selfish choice of consumers acting through the market have led society far astray—as the growth of the tobacco and automobile industries has demonstrated. Clearly, the trends of technological development must be brought under central social control to serve social ends that are set forth in long-run social plans. Most of our more important social problems can be solved only through enlightened social policy, seldom by the market alone.

The first successful socialist economy, the highly centralized and dictatorial model of the Soviet Union, was itself a revolutionary adaptation of social, political, and economic relations to changing technologies and away from obsolete institutions that had created intolerable conditions in Czarist Russia. That model produced not only a new form of society that was able to survive despite all efforts to destroy it, but one capable of sustained growth at unprecedented rates. It is still capable, because it generates such vast resources for investment, of producing under some conditions high rates of increase of gross product, and even of economic standards of living. But it has frozen its social and political development at the stage of the "dictatorship of the proletariat," and this is entirely unnecessary for people who have liquidated the internal class enemy. It is not only unnecessary but insulting to an increasingly educated people loyal to the ideals of socialism. Maintenance of dictation beyond the minimum time essential for it not only alienates people from socialism, it also tends to introduce elements of stagnation into the economy. The centralized model becomes an increasing drag on efficient economic development and upon technological innovation.

Important innovations that relate to economic management and improved incentives could be introduced even within the centralized model, and not a few experiments are being tried in socialist economics. It is practically a tautology to assert that the efficiency of an economic system depends in large part on the effectiveness of its incentives for efficient work and management. As societies advance we can expect that they will rely increasingly on moral incentives and less on economic self-interest. But at this stage of development it is folly to expect that moral incentives will prevail over economic counterincentives to efficiency, such as basing the classification of the enterprise and the salaries of the management upon the number of workers employed, or the linking of bonuses to the amount spent for wages! When managers and workers were allowed to share in the savings arising from increased productivity the results have often been spectacular. At the Shchekino chemical plant in the Soviet Union, when incentives were changed to reward increased efficiency, the productivity of labor rose 86.6 percent in two years! *(Voprosy Ekonomiki,* No. 10, 1969, p. 38.) The question arises, why have the countries with highly centralized models of management been so slow in removing these blocks to efficiency? As the Shchekino experiment proved, solutions are available that are fully compatible with socialism. For answers we must turn to the political side of the problem.

A political bureaucracy without effective competition is slow in responding either to consumer needs, to the need for efficiency of management, or (with notable exceptions) to the advantages of new technologies. The centralized model, once a revolutionary innovation and promoting other revolutionary developments, itself becomes obsolete and a brake to the changes required by new production techniques. Under the more advanced conditions it creates it becomes overcentralized. The changes away from the centralized model necessarily are political as well as economic and, for completely understandable reasons, tend to be feared and resisted by a bureaucracy that has become accustomed to use of its power to stifle criticism and to manufacture self-praise. This is the nub of the matter and this is the ultimate heresy: the Communist Party itself needs competition.

A complex society cannot be planned and managed entirely from the center. With millions of items and billions of production, political, and social decisions to be made, the center is simply overwhelmed if it attempts to concentrate too much decision-making in its own hands. Overcentralization almost always develops under a bureaucratic regime, but it also overwhelms the bureaucracy which seeks refuge in rules and regulations that cannot meet the

Aftermath—But No Epitaph   169

needs of an evolving society. The bureaucracy becomes more and more involved in detail that it cannot cope with, it has less time for important problems, for formulating vital long-range social policies. Some measure of decentralization and division of the decision-making function must be carried out; the factory managers must make most of the operating decisions, the market must be used as a *guide* to the quantities, kinds, and qualities of commodities and services to be produced. At times the market must be overruled to conform to general social policy, but much of the economic plan can be built up directly from market information without specifying production details.

The central planners must have time to consider and determine basic policy in regard to the proportion of investment to consumption, the adequacy of medical service, and similar fundamental questions. They cannot do this if they are concerned with such things as the style and color of shirts. It would be enough to see that appropriate materials and other resources are available and not wasted. The planners must see that the economic incentives are compatible with moral incentives and that they continuously improve efficiency and protect quality.

In weighing the balance of centralization and decentralization of power the political advantages of democracy must not be forgotten, for these advantages relate not only to the motivation of people while they are acting as producers, they relate to their development and quality as citizens. Democracy needs practice. It must be used to the greatest extent possible in all spheres of society if it is to flourish in the political. An increasingly educated people will be increasingly discontent with dictation in areas in which they are competent to decide. . . . And never fear, there will be plenty of acutely difficult problems to keep the central authorities and governmental agencies busy if they confine themselves to those which only they can resolve.

Our final conclusion is: Advancing science and technology create complex social problems that increasingly demand central decision-making and planning in order to protect the social interest, but at the same time the increasing complexity of modern economies requires that more of the decision-making be delegated to the lowest level compatible with adopted social policies. In order to cope with the problems of advanced societes we must use both central planning and a competitive market, and we must do so in the most democratic manner that is feasible. Each country has different problems and must find its own solutions that fit its own specific characteristics, but these general principles will hold.

I submit that the Czechoslovak people in 1968 were trying to advance their society in line with these principles and within the framework of a democratic socialism. They have been suppressed and blocked in their pioneer effort, but that effort was not in vain and their ideas will not die because they were in full conformity with the necessities of development of human relations today.

Index

Academy of Sciences, Czechoslovak, xiii, 117, 149, 160, 163
Action Program, xiii, 128, 139–40, 141–48
Agricultural Commission of the Party Central Committee, 129
Agriculture, 7, 23, 28–32, 36, 47–48, 92, 95, 97–98, 103, 129
Alaska, xii, 98
Alienation, 4, 24, 58, 65, 103, 114, 118–21
American Federation of Labor, 2
Austria, 46

B-52 bombers, 98
Baibakov, N., 83–84
Baťa, 100
Bauer, Adolf, 30
Belozerova, Z., 76
Beneš, Eduard, 9–10, 14
Benešov, Bohemia, 149
Berger, Wolfgang, 68–70
Beria, 121–22, 159
Berle, A., 67
Bilák, Vasil, 163
Bohemia, 7–8, 116, 120
Bojarski, 122
Bratislava, 157, 163
Bratislava Agreement, 157–58, 160
Brazil, 123
"Brezhnev doctrine," 156–57
Brezhnev, Leonid, 47–48, 153, 156–58, 164
Brno, 92
Brus, W., 65
Bulgaria, 153, 157–58
Bureaucracy, 12, 21, 65, 72, 83–86, 91, 93, 97, 100–02, 104, 111, 116, 118, 124, 126, 128, 130, 142, 151, 154, 168
Burnham, James, 67

California Gold Rush of 1849, 89
Canada, 98
Catholic religion, 7, 114
Censorship, xiii, 93–94, 116–18, 122, 142, 154, 162
Central Commission of People's Control and Statistics, 137
Central Committee of the Czechoslovak Communist Party, 100, 111, 119, 122, 132, 137, 138–39, 140, 143, 145, 149, 155, 161, 163
Central Committee for Statistics and Control, 110
Central Control Commission of the Communist Party, 122

Centralized model (of economy), 9, 11–20, 23–24, 27, 31, 39, 59–61, 64, 66–71, 77–78, 83, 89–90, 124, 142, 146, 162
Čepička, Alexej, 123
Černík, Oldřich, 133, 136, 161
Chalupský, Z., 45
Change (innovation), 1–5, 38, 165–66; uninterrupted, frontispiece
Charles University, 7, 127, 155
Chauvinism, great-nation, 165
Chicago, xii, 109
China, 157
C.I.A., 134
Čierná nad Tisou, 157
Cisař, Čestmír, 119, 163
Class struggle, 8, 12–13, 16, 17, 120, 124, 141–42
"Club 231," 154
CMEA (also COMECON), 164
Cold war, xiii, 15, 100, 101
COMECON (or CMEA), 45, 81, 164
Comenius, Jan Amos, 7
Comenius University, 163
Commander in Chief of the Army, 132
Commodity production, 20
Communist Party, USSR, 107, 121–22, 124–25, 142, 153, 156–58, 164
Competition, between socialism and capitalism, 3, 145, 150, 166; in agriculture, 30; market, 7, 10, 55, 66, 68–69, 71–74, 99
Computers, 78, 83
Constitution of 1920, 8
Construction, 61–63
Consumption, 25–27, 32, 56, 69–70
Controls, administrative, 114–16, 119
Cooperatives, 29–31, 90–91, 95
Cost accounting, 44, 96–101
"Cost plus," 49–51, 98–99
Council of Ministers of the USSR, 77
"Counter-revolution," xi, 134, 136, 141, 156, 161
Culture, 3, 4, 7–8, 126–28, 143
Cycle, economic crisis, 8, 61
Czechoslovak National Council, 137

Decentralization, 22, 82, 95, 112, 146–47
Decision-making, 108, 139
Democracy, xi, 24, 58, 130, 133, 135, 137–38, 139–41, 145–47, 156
Denison, E. F., 4

171

172 INDEX

Deputy Minister of Agriculture, 137
Dialectics, 2
Dictatorship of the proletariat, xi, 2, 10–16, 65, 104, 119–20, 124–25, 128, 130, 141
Distant Early Warning, 98
Dogmatism, 21, 65, 149
Dolanský, Jaromír, 48, 100
Dominican Republic, 156
Dresden, 153
Dubček, Alexander, 127, 132, 136, 139–40, 153, 155, 161, 163
Dulles, John Foster, 15

Ecology, 166–67
Economic Institute, Czechoslovak Academy of Sciences, xiii, 111
Education, 7–8, 11, 101–07, 130
Efficiency, 2, 20, 33, 39–48, 52, 53, 62, 71–72
Egypt, 74
Eichhorn, Wolfgang, 30
Einstein, Albert, 1
Eisler, Pavel, 18
Eleventh Congress of the Communist Party of the Soviet Union, 106
Employment, 37, 61–63
Engels, Frederick, frontispiece, 2, 16, 20
England, xii, 88
Estonian Republic, 97
Europe, 149

Fierlinger, Zdeněk, 9
First Five-Year Plan, 100
First Republic, Czechoslovak, 103
First Secretary of Communist Party, 132, 142
Flek, Josef, 8, 9, 10–11
Fourteenth Congress of the Party, 142, 158, 160
France, 147, 155
Freedom, and socialism, 16, 24, 162; private enterprise, 90–91
Frejka, Ludvík (Dr.), 18

Galbraith, J. K., 67–68, 83
German Democratic Republic, G.D.R. (East Germany), 30, 44–46, 90, 153, 157–58, 162
Germany (West), xii, 25, 27, 46, 149
Gestapo, 159
Gillette, 87
Goldmann, Josef, 9–11, 18–19, 25, 27, 55–56, 65
Goldstücker, Eduard, 127–28, 163
Gomulka, W., 162
Gottwald, Klement, 9–10, 15, 122

Great Britain, 93, 98, 127, 149, 159
Griffith, W. E., 79
Gross national product, 26
Growth, economic, 3–4, 25–27, 65

Hájek, Bedřich, 159
Hájek, Jiří, 149, 159, 163
Hardesty, John, 166
Hayek, F. A. von, 22
Hejzlar, Zdeněk, 119
Hendryck, Jiří, 131
Housing policy, 28
Humanistic Mission of Culture, 143
Hungary, 120, 153, 157–58
Husák, Gustav (Dr.), 163
Hussites, 6

Incentives, motivation, 4, 7, 9, 24, 28, 65, 74, 81, 83–96, 105, 145
Income, 35, 37
Indra, Alois, 163
Industrial development, 32–36
Industrial Revolution, 2
Innovation, change, 1–2, 4–5, 24, 38, 61, 75, 81–82, 87–89, 103
Institute for History of the Communist Party, 122
Integration, economic, 164–65
International Brigade in Spain, 123, 155
International Trade Fair at Brno, 92
Intervention, government, 66; military, 151–58, 160
Invasion (August 1968), xiii, 158
Investment, 26, 39, 40–48, 65
Izvestia, 159–60

Japan, xii, 25
Jawa plant, 86
Jews, 122
Johnson, W. A., 166

Kaplan, K., 120, 122
Karpeles, 159
Kendrick, John W., 47
Khrushchev, 126
Kiev, USSR, 76
Klacek, Jan, 55
Klement Gottwald Military Academy, 133
Klement Gottwald Steel Works in Ostrava, 88
Kopecký, Václav, 123
Kormorov, Y., 164
Košice Program, 9, 133
Kouba, Karel, 55–56, 65
Kral, Karel, 25, 27–28
Krejčí, Jaroslav, 26
Kreysa, Václav, 100

Kriegel, František (Dr.), 155, 161, 163
Krylov, P., 70–71
Kutná Hora, 149
Kuznets, Simon, 4
Kvaša, Y., 98

Lab, Miroslav, 113
Lange, Oscar, 22, 79
Lansberg, Hans, 47
Latvia, 84
Laws, economic, 27, 44, 47, 68–69
"Leading role" of Communist Party, 3, 102, 106–07, 109, 113, 134, 139, 140–41, 150, 157–58, 160, 162–63
Lenin, V. I., 2, 20–21, 97, 106–07, 115, 165
Leontyev, L., 27
Liehm, Antonín J., 126–27
Likhachev, 121–22
Literacy, 7–8
Loebl, Eugene, 121
Lomsky, Bohumír, 132
London, Artur, 121

"Make-work," 95, 98, 104
Management, 3, 7, 11–12, 28, 47, 48, 65–66, 70, 86, 97–98, 142, 144–47, 165; "new system," 76, 84, 113, 126–50
Management on works councils, 28
Makarov, 121
Market, 7, 10, 19–20, 22, 66–72, 81, 82–83, 94–95, 146
Marx, Karl, 2
Marxism, 149, 151; -Leninism, 155
Masaryk, Thomas G., 7, 102
Material balances, 18–19
McCarthy, Joseph, 16
McNamara, Robert, 98
Means, G., 67
Medical care, 11, 28
Military, xi
Militia, workers', 10, 14; see also People's Militia
Mináč, Vladimír, 161
Ministries, xii, 9, 77–78, 101, 109–10, 112, 133, 147–48
Mises, Ludwig von, 22
Momet, V., 77
Monopoly, 7, 64, 73–75
Morale, 49
Moravia, 7, 133
Munich agreement, 8, 149

National Committees, 113, 130
National Front, 13, 109, 140, 155
National income, 35, 36–37, 39–47
National Museum, 162
Nationalization, 9–10, 30, 112
Nazis, 8–9, 133, 137
"New System," 126–50, 151
New York, 126
Nixon, Richard M., 15
North Africa, 147
Novotný, Antonín, 58, 93, 118, 123–24, 126, 129, 130–33, 139–40, 151, 154, 163

Orlov, Yuri Alexandrovitch, 160
Ostrava School of Mining and Steel Engineering, 133
Ostrava, Moravia, 76, 88, 133
Ownership, social, 16, 66, 71; private, 17, 66, 120–21, 152

Parkinson (Professor), 64, 89
Parliament (National Assembly), 12–13, 109, 110, 133, 137, 140, 147, 155, 157, 160, 163
Party discipline, 139–40
Pavel, Josef, 122, 147–48, 161, 163
Pentagon, 98
People's Commissariat of Workers and Peasants Inspection, 115
People's Militia, 10, 14, 147, 155, 160–61
PERT, 98
"Petty tutelage," 93, 105, 126, 129, 162
Plan targets, 23; quantity, 75–78, 81, 98
Planning, 7, 16–21, 24–27, 61, 63–64, 66–71, 147
Planning Office, 110
Pléva, Ján, 55–56
Plzeň, 112
Poland, 44–45, 93, 121, 153, 157, 162
Pollution, 165–66
Potsdam agreement, 15
Power, structure of, 108–26
Prague, 86–87, 91, 92, 95, 99, 119, 126, 137, 153, 155, 159
Presidium of the Central Committee, 131, 140, 149
Prices and pricing, 9, 21–22, 35, 44, 73–74, 75, 80–84, 97, 98–99
Private enterprise, 90–91, 120–21
Productivity, 3–4, 18–19, 32, 35–36, 56–59, 61–63, 84

Quality, 75–77, 79, 88

Racism, 143
Rationing, 22–23
Reed College, xii
Reinhold, Otto, 68–70

INDEX

Responsibility, 108, 111–12, 113
Richta, Radovan, 3
Risk and incentives, 4, 76, 79, 83–96
Robbins, Lionel, 22
Rosa Luxemburg knitting mill, 76
Rožmberk Castle, 116

Schumpeter, Joseph, 83
Science and development, 3, 4, 7, 52, 69–70, 117, 144–45, 149, 152; in agriculture, 30–32
Secrecy, 100
Security, 28, 36, 72
Šejna, Jan, 132
Senate (U.S.) Foreign Relations Committee, 15
Shchekino chemical plant, 168
"Shop on Main Street, The," 118
Šik, Ota, 20, 57–58, 65, 69–70, 79, 111, 119, 152, 163
Široký, Vilém, 123
Sitnin, V., 79–82
Sixth Congress of Unified Agricultural Cooperatives (April 23–26, 1964), 93–94
Škoda, 112
Slansky trial, 121, 122
Slovak Uprising, 161, 163
Slovakia, 96, 127, 132, 133, 148, 161; eastern, 157
Slovaks, 89, 137, 139, 150, 161–63
Smrkovský, Josef, 137, 138, 161, 163
Social costs, 99
Social Security system, 110
Socialist emulation, 28, 49
Sokol sports organization, 123
Solow, Robert M., 4
South America, 160
Sovereignty, 8, 156, 158, 160, 164–65
Soviet Union, 8–9, 11, 14, 17, 45–46, 54, 56, 81, 83–84, 97–98, 101, 106–07, 132, 133, 138, 149, 153, 155, 156–59, 164, 165, 167
Špaček, Josef, 149
Stagnation, 4–5, 23, 39, 73
Stalin, Joseph, 13, 15, 17, 114, 122, 124–25, 149
State Bank, 110
State Committee on Prices of the USSR State Planning Committee, 79–82
State Planning Board (GOSPLAN), 77, 79, 83, 100
Storming, 48–49, 51
Students, 128, 131
Subsidies, 21, 55, 96–97
Svoboda, Ludvík (General), 133, 148, 163

Tábor, 6, 103
Táborský, Edward, 14
Tass, 158
Technology, 2–4, 24, 25, 46, 59–60, 61, 66, 72, 74, 92, 166–67
Thirteenth Party Congress, 129–31
Trade Unions, 10, 110
Trials, political, 120–23, 148
Trotskyite conspirators, 121
Twelfth Congress of the Communist Party, 128–29
Twentieth Congress of the Communist Party of the Soviet Union, 142
Twenty-fourth Congress of the (Soviet) Communist Party, 164
"Two Thousand Words," 134–37, 138, 154

Úklid, 91
Ukraine, 77
Ulbricht, 162
Unemployment, 8, 20, 36
Union of Czechoslovak Youth, 149
Union Republic Ministry, 77
Union of Slovak Writers, 161
United Nations, 149, 159
United Nations Security Council, 159
United States, 89, 98, 105, 109, 156, 162
United States Department of Agriculture, 117
Urválek, Jiří, 122
Usenko, Y. I., 165

Vaculík, Ludvík, 126, 134
Velenka, Bohemia, 137
Vietnam, 98, 156
Vitásek, 115–16
Vitkovice, 76; steel mill, 133
Volvochenko, Ivan, 47, 97
Voronezh, 97

Wages, real, 24
War criminals, 8
Warsaw, xi, 153, 155, 156
Warsaw-Brezhnev doctrine, 153, 155–57, 160, 164
Warsaw Pact, 153, 157–58, 160
Waste, of capacity, 48–49, 51; of materials, 52–56
Wheeler, George S., xii–xiv, 3, 73
Workers' councils, 146
World War I, 98, 133
World War II, 132
Writers Congress, 131
Writers' Union, 126–27

Zhukov, Yuri, 152
Zhdanov, A. A., 127